JUDO
Skills and Techniques

"JUDO
Skills and Techniques"

TONY "REAY", 6th DAN

THE CROWOOD PRESS

First published in 1985 by
THE CROWOOD PRESS
Crowood House, Ramsbury
Marlborough, Wiltshire SN8 2HE

Reprinted, 1986
Paperback edition, 1986

British Library Cataloguing in Publication Data

Reay, Tony
    Judo : skills and techniques.—(Crowood sports books)
    1. Judo
    I. Title
    796.8' 152   GV1114
    ISBN 0-946284-22-9

Acknowledgements

Action photographs by David Finch

Cover shot by David Finch

Line illustrations by Tony Reay

Series Adviser David Bunker, Lecturer, Loughborough University

Typeset by Inforum Ltd, Portsmouth
Printed and bound by Robert Hartnoll Ltd., Bodmin, Cornwall

Contents

Tony Reay, 6th Dan, is Development Officer for the British Judo Association. He has been involved with judo for thirty years, gained 1st Dan in 1959 and, weighing just over 10 stone, represented Great Britain at a time when there were no weight categories – a remarkable achievement. He is editor of *British Judo* and co-author of the *Judo Manual.*

Tony Reay is the best all-round judo instructor of all levels, both sexes, and all ages, I have ever seen, and this book encapsulates his vast experience.

John Goodbody

Tony Reay has put into print his unquestionably profound knowledge of judo. Anyone interested in judo will, I am sure, benefit from reading this book.

Arthur Mapp, National Squads Manager

Two of the good things about being an international competitor are the opportunity to wear the British International badge and the many different countries around the world you are able to visit.

In my travels, the very high standard of British judo and the respect and admiration others have for our judo instructors and administrators has been brought home to me. For many years the British Judo Association has had a policy whereby ex-competitors are encouraged to continue as coaches and administrators. I now realise that it is people like Tony Reay who have continued to build on firm foundations and made British judo what it is today.

Judo is now no longer a minor sport in Britain, and our international competitors have made judo one of Britain's most successful sports. It is thanks to the author and his contemporaries who have given us the opportunity to obtain those successes.

Neil Adams, MBE

Introduction

Judo is a training for life. These are not my words, they are the words of the founder of judo, Professor Jigoro Kano (1860–1938). In 1882 Professor Kano created from the ancient art of *ju-jitsu* what is now often described as 'the modern combat sport of judo'. Kano was a forward thinking man and, with the dramatic social and political changes that were taking place all around him in Japan at the time, he could see that many of those former ju-jitsu skills could be lost forever. Professor Kano was also concerned with physical education in schools in his country and he felt he needed something with a Japanese flavour to interest his people.

Thus Professor Kano created his Kodokan Judo as he called it. As a result we now have a world-wide modern Olympic sport practised by millions of people and gaining popularity year by year. It is not surprising therefore that we in judo do tend to look upon Kano with a reverence bordering on the divine. He was the Founder, the Messiah, the man who gave so much involvement and enjoyment to many. There are many of us who would go so far as to say he has given a new meaning to life. To suggest that judo is a training for life may seem to the reader to be overdoing things somewhat. To those who have never before made a study of judo it may seem to be a pretentious claim. If you are one of those people I hope you will not dismiss such claims before you have had a good look at what judo is really all about. I hope that this book will give you a better understanding and, who knows, you yourself might even become another judo enthusiast when you have read and studied these pages. Perhaps by then you also will see that judo does indeed reflect the 'ups and downs' of life. Perhaps by then you will understand why judo has been described as 'a preparation for life'.

APPEAL

There is a place for everyone in judo. It is an activity for all ages, for male or female, it cuts across all classes and creeds, it caters for both the extrovert and the introvert – even the disabled can become involved. There are those who study judo purely for judo's sake; the vast range of techniques and skills appeal to them. There are those who practise judo as a means of keeping fit. The beginner will find that other forms of training such as weight-training are not really necessary. It is only the top level competitors who find the need for such extra training, and that is only because usually they cannot find sufficient partners of their own standard to practise with. Judo has its own set of built-in exercises. There are those who do like to be involved in the 'competition' aspect of judo and want to reach up and attain the contest honours that now abound at tournaments of every level from club to international standard. There are also those who look upon judo as more than just a physical activity; to them it is more than just a sport, it is an art form to be studied in great depth. Such people spend hours honing their particular techniques to the finest degree. Finally, there are those who look upon judo as a method of self-defence. It is my hope that this book will help all those people.

OBJECT

The technical object of judo is quite simple to understand. The idea is to overcome another person without having any advantage other than your own skill, strength and resourcefulness. This means that *judoka* (people who practise judo) compete with each other on equal terms, without weapons and, for safety, within a set of rules. The object is to attempt to outwit and out manoeuvre an opponent and throw him onto the ground, or immobilise or gain a submission from him before he can do likewise to you – all without incurring injury. I have often heard judo described as a physical game of chess – and I think that sums it up quite nicely.

WRESTLING STYLES

There have been many different wrestling styles down the ages and in different parts of the world. Some have survived to become accepted sports in the modern world. Some survive in the backwaters of local communities and some have become extinct. There are naked styles of wrestling, such as Greco Roman, where grips and holds can be applied only on the body. There are belt styles, such as Glima wrestling (Iceland) or Sumo wrestling (Japan), in which the grips and purchase are made primarily on the opponent's belt. Then there are the styles where full clothing is in use, such as Sambo (Soviet Union) and Judo (Japan), and these therefore offer a greater range of grips.

Range of Techniques

On the basis that so many more techniques can be applied in judo because of the many uses that can be made of the *judogi* (judo suit), it can be said to transcend all the other styles. The judogi comprises a reinforced jacket, a belt and trousers. The trousers are also usually reinforced at the knees. In judo there is not only a wide range of throwing techniques, but there are also techniques that can be employed on the ground. Many of these, and the arm-locks and strangles that can be used both in standing judo and judo on the ground, cannot be found in the other wrestling styles.

Winning is important in judo whether you are having a *randori* (practice) with a friend or whether you are competing in a *shiai* (contest), but the development of winning techniques must be by far the most important goal to aim for. The beginner must try to start out correctly, by developing skill, and by working on technique. You cannot develop a skilful technique within ten or a dozen lessons, you must work at the movement until it becomes part of you. When you can do the overall movement without being conscious of it, without having to think about the parts, then you are on the way to perfection. That is not all, however; you then have to learn how and when you can apply that technique. You will only learn this through regular practice and experience. This book is designed to help the reader on the way to attaining skill, but in the last resort it is all down to you and the effort you put into training.

TERMINOLOGY

Judo is universal. Kodokan judo is the same throughout the world. There are no different schools or styles as with other martial arts, such as karate. Because judo was originally Japanese we use Japanese terminology. There have been efforts in the past to dispense with the Japanese terminology. In some countries the different techniques were numbered, and in many countries the techniques have been translated and described in the mother tongue. 'Why should you have to learn a language when all you want to do is learn a sport', has often been the question. That is a very good argument, but the fact is people who take up judo and want to become part of the judo fraternity do actually like to use the Japanese terms. *O-soto-gari* conveys to the judoka a specific judo throw. Translated into English it means 'major outer reaping', which does not describe what the actual throw is, so the original Japanese may as well be used. I have found that people starting judo find the use of Japanese quite fascinating, and in using the Japanese terms they begin to feel they are part of the judo family. From a coaching point of view it should not matter too much whether a competitor calls it *o-soto-gari* or major outer reaping, provided he can do it well and skilfully and that it is a 'match-winner'. The rules in international judo have broadened and have become quite complex and so both referees and international competitors do need a good understanding of the Japanese terms. It is for this reason that this book uses Japanese terms, and if the reader is not too sure, there is always the glossary of judo terms at the back of the book which can be refered to when nobody else is looking.

Judo can be most rewarding. It has so much depth one can never really feel one has covered everything – there is always something more. It is, however, a tough and demanding activity, let there be no mistake about that. But it is the challenge that appeals to many people. Nothing is worth attaining if it is too easily acquired, and on that note I return to the opening theme. Judo is very much like life.

1 History

ANCIENT ROOTS

Jigoro Kano lived during a period of dramatic change and upheaval in his country. These revolutionary changes were both social and political. It was a period after which the Japanese, having for so many centuries isolated themselves from the rest of the world, were economically and politically forced to open their ports and trading posts to traders from across the seas.

Up to that great period of change ju-jitsu was a brutal and often lethal method of fighting, and there had been many schools spe-cialising in these skills scattered throughout Japan. Ju-jitsu goes back many centuries in Japanese history and its origin is vague. Early records refer to trials of strength and skills under a number of different names such as *yawara,* but which eventually became commonly known as ju-jitsu.

During this changing process Kano had been concerned about the standard of physical education in Japanese schools compared to that in the Western world. In forming his Kodokan Judo from the various schools of ju-jitsu, he collected many techniques which were eventually to form his system. Perhaps

Fig 1 Judo is derived from the ancient art of ju-jitsu.

the greatest aspect of his judo system was *randori,* and one wonders if even he realised how successful this feature would be. It is interesting to note that he never suggested that his judo system was a sport. In launching his Kodokan Judo in 1882, Kano gave to the world a new combat activity derived and updated from the ancient fighting arts of Japan. Eighty-two years later this system was being recognised around the world as an Olympic combat sport.

SPREAD OF JUDO

It was not long before a number of Kano's pupils began to export his judo overseas. In many countries it was received with great interest, and from 1900 to 1905 there are reports of courses and demonstrations taking place in such cities as Budapest, London and New York. It appears, however, that for quite some time little effort was made to distinguish between judo and ju-jitsu in the Western press. Many regarded the two as being the same thing, and in a sense they were. Kano's pupils may have compounded the belief that they were one and the same, for they, like him, had originally studied ju-jitsu.

Kano himself, ever active and mindful of the valuable ideals sport can offer, joined the Olympic movement in 1909, and for the next 29 years was the Japanese Olympic representative. His first visit to Europe and to the United States in the interests of judo was in 1889 and from then onwards he was almost constantly travelling and, in fact, was returning by sea to Japan from such a visit when he died in 1938. Many of his pupils who took judo overseas were to face extreme hardships. Some succumbed to the lure of the music halls of that period by taking on all-comers and earning attractive purses.

BUDOKWAI

The first judo club in Europe was opened in London in 1918. This was the Budokwai (The Way of Knighthood Society) and was founded by Gunji Koizumi (1885–1965). The Budokwai still thrives today, and for many years entire British judo teams consisted of Budokwai members. As a boy, Koizumi studied kenjutsu at school, and later he studied ju-jitsu. It was much later when he actually joined the Kodokan. Convinced that judo was a discipline for physical, mental and moral training, it became for him 'The Way'. Koizumi visited several countries before settling in England. He loved England and visited the places of interest, the museums, and the English countryside whenever he could. In his appearance and manner he was gentle to the extreme, and when teaching judo he demonstrated enormous patience. He had great courage and strong determination, and he was eventually to be the architect of Kano's greatest dream, the formation of a federation of judo associations of various countries. In 1948 Koizumi was instrumental in forming the British Judo Association, and within just a matter of weeks a number of leading judoka from other European countries gathered in London at his invitation to form the European Judo Union. This led the way to the formation of a federation of judo nations from around the world, and in 1952 the International Judo Federation came into being. In 1962 the Kodokan awarded Koizumi the judo grade of 8th Dan and up to his death on his eightieth birthday he continued to visit his beloved Budokwai. In a small garden on the Chelsea embankment in London can be found a Japanese cherry tree, at the base of which is a small brass plaque dedicated to the memory of 'The father of British Judo'.

INTERNATIONAL JUDO FEDERATION

The International Judo Federation (IJF) is composed of national governing bodies which are affiliated to the five continental Unions, and it recognises as judo that which was created by Jigoro Kano. Among others, the aims of the IJF are to promote cordial and friendly relations between its members and to organise and promote judo throughout the world. Apart from spreading the techniques and spirit of judo, a most important function of the IJF is to establish international regulations of judo. Judo has perhaps been fortunate, in that there is only one style or school, and this one style is the same throughout the world.

COMPETITION

The First World Judo Championships were held in Tokyo in 1956. Weight categories, as were commonly accepted in boxing and wrestling, had still not been considered for judo. Indeed, many judoka at that time would have reacted in horror at the mere suggestion. There was still the misguided notion that a good little 'un could beat a good big 'un. It is true that judo has a lot to offer the small judoka, but his skills, against a bigger opponent with the same skills, are cancelled out by the weight and strength of the bigger man. A small judoka can only be impressive against a bigger opponent when the bigger opponent is less skilful. This point is borne out when we look at the winners of the first three World Championships, which were open-weight events; they were all very big – albeit very skilful – competitors.

Weight Categories

Japan was to host the 1964 Olympic Games and wished to include judo in the programme. The International Olympic Committee (IOC) agreed, but only if the competition were to be organised in weight categories in order that medal winning opportunities were available to a greater proportion of countries. The 1964 Olympic Games judo event was therefore fought out in four weight categories which included an open-weight category.

In the Fourth World Championships the following year the same weight categories were used. These were; Under 68 kilos, Under 80 kilos. Over 80 kilos and the Open-weight division. The weight categories in the 1967 World Championships were increased to six, including the Open class.

The IOC had been satisfied that the 1964 Olympic Games had shown that there was sufficient world-wide interest and involvement in judo, and although it was not to figure in the 1968 Games in Mexico, thereafter it was firmly established on the Olympic programme.

At the Eleventh World Championships held in Paris in 1979 the weights were increased to seven, plus an Open category, and they remain so today. The categories are Under 60 kilos (-60 kg), Under 65 kilos (-65 kg), Under 71 kilos (-71 kg), Under 78 kilos (-78 kg), Under 86 kilos (-86 kg), Under 95 kilos (-95 kg) and Over 95 kilos (+95 kg).

Women's Judo

In 1980 the First World Championships for women were held. Women's judo had been on the international scene seven or eight years earlier, starting out with matches between countries and then, as in Europe in 1975, continental competitions. It was only when tournaments were being held in all five continents that the IJF would agree to staging a World Championships for women.

At the First World Championships for women, held in New York Madison Square

Gardens, the categories were Under 48 kilos (-48 kg), Under 52 kilos (-52 kg), Under 61 kilos (-61 kg), Under 66 kilos (-66 kg), Under 72 kilos (-72 kg) and Over 72 kilos (+72 kg).

With these first World Championships for women having taken place there is just one more hurdle for the women in their claim for equal status in international competition to overcome, that is for women's judo to be included on the Olympic Games programme.

RECENT RESULTS

Japan did not take part in the 1980 Olympic Games, but for the scholar of judo the results make interesting reading when comparing the rest of the world's competitors. At these Games the Soviet Union and France took two Golds each. Ezio Gamba of Italy won the 71 kg category on a decision in the final against Neil Adams of Great Britain. Jurg Rothlisberger of Switzerland won the -86 kg title, with Robert Van de Walle of Belgium winning the +95 kg and Dietmar Lorenz of the German Democratic Republic the Open.

With Neil Adams winning a Silver medal and Arthur Mapp a Bronze in the Open, Britain maintained an impressive Olympic medal-winning record. The United States was another country which had boycotted these Games but, despite the large following of judo enthusiasts in that country, the USA has made little impression down the years in Olympic and World tournaments. In the 1964 Games James Bregman from Washington D.C. took a Bronze and in the 1976 Games Allen Coage won a Bronze. They have had special political problems within their judo administration and, once these have been sorted out, there is no reason to suppose that they will not do better. At the 1983 World Championships and the 1984 Olympic Games they made their presence felt and once the American machine

gets into gear we could see some good results from the Western hemisphere.

The 1981 World Championships for Men were held in Maastricht in Holland, and it was there that the great Yasuhiro Yamashita of Japan accomplished a feat never before achieved in the history of the championships. He won both the -95 kg and Open categories. Neil Adams won Britain's first world title in the -78 kg. For many years Korean competitors have lived in the shadow of their Japanese neighbours, but at this event Chong Hak Park of South Korea won the -71 kg. Bernard Tchoullouyon of France won the -86 kg title and Tengis Khubuluri of the Soviet Union the -95 kg. The other titles went to Yasuhiko Moriwaki in the -60 kg and Katsuhiko Kashiwazaki in the -65 kg for Japan.

The Thirteenth World Championships for Men took place in Moscow in 1983 and, with the Japanese again involved, the results make interesting reading. Khazret Tletseri and Nikolai Solodukhin, both of the Soviet Union, won the -60 kg and -65 kg categories. Hidetoshi Nakanishi of Japan won the -71 kg and his fellow countryman Nobutoshi Hikage won the -78 kg. Detlef Ultsch won the -86 kg and Anreas Preschel, both of the German Democratic Republic, won the -95 kg. The famous Yamashita of Japan won the +95 kg and Hitoshi Saito, also of Japan, won the Open.

The 1984 Olympic Games in Los Angeles was plagued with a boycott. This time the Soviet Union, German Democratic Republic and other Eastern bloc countries did not take part, and this was bound to have an effect on the medal table.

Shinji Hosokawa of Japan got his country off to a good start in the -60 kg category. Yoshiyuki Matsuoka of Japan then won the -65 kg but it was a Korean, Byeong-keun Ahn, who took the -71 kg title. In the -78 kg category, Neil Adams of Great Britain was making his second bid for an Olympic Gold medal, but a comparative unknown, Frank Wieneke of the Federal Republic of Germany, beat him in the final. Peter Seisenbacher of Austria won the -86 kg title and Hyoung-Zoo Ha of Korea won the -95 kg. Hitoshi Saito of Japan won the +95 kg category and, despite a serious leg injury sustained during the tournament, Yasuhiro Yamashita of Japan won the Open. And so, the Japanese were able to wrest again from the rest of the world half the titles available, but it is interesting to note that in those weights where they did not win a title the Japanese came nowhere at all in the medals.

The story continues and with each succeeding year becomes more interesting. Around the world judo becomes more popular, but what of Japan? It is sometimes said that they no longer display the same fanatical approach to their training. With their new-found wealth and adoption of Western ways are they perhaps becoming too soft? This was what the *Senseis* (teachers) of the old school feared. Perhaps they were right after all.

2 The Grading Structure

The grading structure is an integral part of judo. It runs through many other aspects of Japanese life, but it is a distinctive feature of judo throughout the world. The judoka wears his or her belt with pride, whatever the colour. The colour denotes the standard he or she has achieved, but whether it be a yellow or a black belt, the judoka wears it with the satisfied inner feeling of having achieved something important.

METHOD OF GRADING

A grading is a promotion examination where a player tests himself against players of the same level and, if he can show superiority, can win himself promotion to the next level or rank. There are two aspects to a grading or promotion examination, firstly the physical test of skills by way of a number of contests, and secondly the test of knowledge.

Belts

The grading structure is rather like a ladder of achievement. The colours of the belts denote the rungs of the ladder. The darker the colour of the belt, the higher the grade. The governing body of judo in each country is responsible for the grade structure of that country. Consequently, structures differ from country to country, as do standards. In Japan, for example, they do not have as many 'steps' or rungs of the ladder in their *Kyu* (senior student) grade structure, nor do they have the many different coloured belts, as are common in European countries. Their 1st Kyus, which

are the top level of the student grades, are not generally as strong or as high a standard as their European counterparts. The *Dan* (leader) grades do, however, level out fairly commonly around the world. It is also interesting to note that the Japanese do not have a junior grading structure and have very little competition for juniors below the age of fifteen years. A phenomenon of British judo is that, over recent years, the annual calendar has become full of competitions for juniors from the age of eight to fifteen years.

The ultimate aim of nearly every judo enthusiast is to achieve his or her 1st Dan black-belt (*Shodan*). There are, however, further steps upwards in the Dan grade or 'leader' division. People are often confused by the fact that some leading competitors are not necessarily very high Dan grades. This is often because the theory requirements of the competitor's country are very severe or, with his heavy training schedule, that competitor has not had the time to study and sit examinations.

There have been a few very exceptional competitors who have achieved as high a level as 6th Dan before retiring from competition but, in general, 5th Dan and onwards are a kind of honorary grade. These are awarded in recognition of general achievements, such as teaching or for work in the administration of judo.

The highest grade that has ever been awarded in judo is 10th Dan (*Judan*), though there is said to be provision for up to 12th. The Japanese always refer to Kano as *Shihan* which means 'master', though there is no indication he was ever graded. Presumably this was because, being the founder of judo, there was nobody to grade him. There have been seven 10th Dans but, at the time of writing, there are none. It is interesting to note that another translation of *Shihan* (though in different Japanese characters) means 'model for others'.

BRITISH GRADES

In Britain, novices or beginners wear a plain white belt. The grading system in Britain is indicated by the colour of belt and markings as shown below.

The grading system is the envy of other sports and activities. Apart from being a measure of personal proficiency, it is a great spur to the judoka to try constantly to do better. On a cold and damp winter's evening it is easy to forego the judo session at the club, but the thought that you might miss some important teaching or special training which could help you at your next grading will urge you to make that extra effort. There is also one more satisfying aspect, once you have gained your grade – whatever it might be – nobody can possibly take it away.

Mon (junior) Grades

1st mon	– white	belt + one	
2nd mon	– white	belt + two	
3rd mon	– white	belt + three	
4th mon	– yellow	belt + one	
5th mon	– yellow	belt + two	
6th mon	– yellow	belt + three	
7th mon	– orange	belt + one	
8th mon	– orange	belt + two	red ½'' wide
9th mon	– orange	belt + three	bar sewn
10th mon	– green	belt + one	on to one
11th mon	– green	belt + two	belt end.
12th mon	– green	belt + three	
13th mon	– blue	belt + one	
14th mon	– blue	belt + two	
15th mon	– blue	belt + three	
16th mon	– brown	belt + one	
17th mon	– brown	belt + two	
18th mon	– brown	belt + three	

Kyu (adult student) Grades

9th	Kyu	– yellow belt
8th	Kyu	– orange belt
7th	Kyu	– orange belt
6th	Kyu	– green belt
5th	Kyu	– green belt
4th	Kyu	– blue belt
3rd	Kyu	– blue belt
2nd	Kyu	– brown belt
1st	Kyu	– brown belt

Dan (adult leader) Grades

1st	Dan	– black belt
2nd	Dan	– black belt
3rd	Dan	– black belt
4th	Dan	– black belt
5th	Dan	– black belt
6th	Dan	– red and white (blocked) belt
7th	Dan	– red and white (blocked) belt
8th	Dan	– red and white (blocked) belt
9th	Dan	– red belt
10th	Dan	– red belt

3 Recreational Judo

Judo is considered by many people to be more than just a sport. Along with the competitive element adopted by Professor Kano, he included a philosophy for life itself. This philosophy can help the individual to cope better with day to day problems, trials and tribulations. Along with the physical training that goes with judo there is much mental application because of the wide range of throwing, groundwork, counter and continuation techniques. Skills and crafts are fast disappearing from industry as the computer and silicon chip take over, but the mind still needs to be stimulated by something. Judo is the kind of activity which demands concentration. You have to think of your techniques and moves and when and how to apply certain tactics, and you have to keep your mind on what the other person is doing or intends to do.

THERAPY

I have also found that judo can be good therapy for business people and professional people who carry the worries and pressures of their work. I have often been told by such people that as soon as they have carried out the ritual standing bow (*tachi-rei*), signalling the commencement of a practice session or a contest, their problems are immediately forgotten. The reason is that one then has to concentrate on the practice or contest in hand and avoid being thrown or defeated in some other way. Once the breakfalls (*ukemi*) have been perfected there should be no fear of being thrown, but nevertheless no one wants

to be thrown as it is a physical and a psychological humiliation. In concentrating on the job in hand, the judoka therefore blocks out all other thoughts and problems from his mind. There are not many other sports which demand such total concentration. I have often had businessmen tell me that after a good training session they have been completely mentally relaxed and refreshed, and ready to face their business problems with a renewed interest.

Judo is also a great leveller. When you look at a group of judoka gathered in the dojo clad in their white judogi, there is no way of telling what their work or background might be. The only mark of distinction is the colour of the belt, which has nothing to do with their outside position. I have in my time seen princes practising with labourers, bank managers practising with clerks, and yes, even Tories practising with socialists, the one not knowing or even caring what the other might be in the outside world, but each having great respect and appreciation of the other's judo. There is among judoka a tremendous camaraderie and feeling of belonging to a special group.

Young people love to wrestle and roll around with each other on the *tatami* (judo mat). The dojo is their natural habitat. In the dojo or in junior competitions, youngsters can give vent to their natural aggressions and do so in a perfectly controlled atmosphere. The special dojo rules and judo etiquette also teaches children good manners and respect for others. These are the virtues I have heard many parents extol in recent years.

Judo has become very popular the world over with young people. In recent years girls have taken it up with the same enthusiasm as boys in some countries. The result is that some clubs and some instructors now devote their time solely to 'junior judo'. The average club, however, still caters for all groups and people of all ages. It is the complete all-round club which caters also for 'recreational judo' as well as 'contest judo'. Obviously, the more mature adult will not have medal-winning aspirations, but the all-round club caters for and welcomes such people.

Challenge

Judo is a tough and vigorous activity, and that is one of its attractions. There are a surprising number of people in this modern world who resent the soft and easy options it offers. It is they who are looking for something physically and mentally demanding, but also rewarding. Such a person is not a masochist, they simply gain an enormous sense of achievement in overcoming something difficult. There is also the appeal of a challenge – judo is a challenge.

There is a particular thrill in winning, but there can be no greater thrill than that which is experienced when winning with a particular skill. Skills cannot be accomplished in six easy lessons and most people realise that. What a wonderful moment it is when, as a result of special attention to a particular movement practised many times over, it suddenly works. You will never be quite the same person again when, with a certain deftness, even cunning, you have thrown your opponent cleanly onto his back. Judo is such that when you do accomplish a good skilful throw, your opponent will be one of the first to congratulate you.

RULES OF CONDUCT

There are two sets of rules in judo. There are the ordinary rules of conduct, commonly referred to as 'dojo rules', which are generally accepted in judo clubs around the world, and then there are the Contest Rules, by which judo contests are governed. In this section I will explain the dojo rules because, though they are not generally published anywhere, they do affect every judoka and indeed should be observed by everybody in a judo club.

I have deliberately not numbered the following dojo rules because each club may have a certain order of priority. Although described as dojo rules, a judoka would also be expected to observe these rules at a competition or wherever judo is being practised. Following each rule I have added a commentary to explain the reasons for such a rule.

Club Rules for Members

Personal Cleanliness

A high standard of personal cleanliness is expected. Apart from the obvious reason of hygiene, unwashed bodies can be offensive to a partner in such a close proximity activity. There is also the greater possibility of germs affecting broken or grazed skin.

Finger-nails

Finger-nails and toe-nails should be pared short and kept clean. Not only can long finger or toe-nails be a hazard to a partner or opponent, they can be very dangerous for the person possessing them. Should an opponent suddenly snatch away his judogi from a grip, such a sudden action could tear back or tear off the finger-nail. Again, the reason for the nails being clean is because of the danger of germs affecting scratched skin.

Judogi

Judogi must be kept clean. The reasons are

as for the first rule.

Hair

Long hair must be tied back securely. Nasty accidents can occur when, again, during a sudden movement long hair can be caught up in the action. Elastic bands are ideal for tying up hair securely.

Jewellery

Jewellery must be removed. Hard or metallic objects in the hair can be extremely dangerous. A gold chain around the neck would not last long in a randori, and even a rounded and smooth wedding ring can cause broken fingers, and at best can cause sudden and extreme pain when performing certain throws, even when strapped and covered with medical tape.

Footwear

Footwear must be worn when off the mat. This is a 'golden oldie' rule of judo, but should be observed even today despite cleaner surroundings due to better floor surfaces. Dust and dirt adhere easily to bare skin and, because much groundwork takes place on the judo mat, the mat should be kept as clean as possible. Most judo clubs are also martial arts clubs in that they cater for various activities of oriental origin. The worst culprits for walking around barefoot are *karateka* (people who practise *karate* (empty-hand fighting)) simply because in karate there is no groundwork, and so they are not aware of the need for perfectly clean mat surfaces. Like most martial arts enthusiasts however, karateka are very responsible people and are considerate of dojo equipment. They will observe this rule when the reasons for it are explained. Judoka generally wear *zori* which are Japanese straw slippers, or they may wear the more easily obtainable rubber slippers of the same design which are commonly termed 'flip-flops'. It is easy to step out of such footwear when stepping onto the mat.

Shoes

Shoes or any kind of footwear must not be worn on the mat. The biggest crime that can be committed in judo is to step onto the mat area wearing ordinary street shoes or footwear of any description. Modern vinyl-covered judo mats are easy to keep clean but, apart from the hygiene aspect, grit attached to the shoe can easily puncture the vinyl covering and, just as with a small tear in the sail of a boat in heavy weather, so a small tear in the mat covering will soon spread during a heavy training session – and soon render the mat dangerous and useless. The wearing of socks on the mat can be dangerous to the person wearing them. Though cushioned for falling, the judo mat surface is actually quite firm to allow for speed and friction. Anyone wearing socks on such a surface will slip quite easily and dangerously. Only in very special circumstances will the wearing of socks be allowed, and only at the discretion of the instructor in charge.

Leaving the Dojo

Members must not leave the dojo without gaining permission from the instructor. This is not a rule designed simply to assert the instructor's authority. It is a very important rule, especially where children are concerned. The instructor is responsible for the people who have been placed in his charge and he should be aware of any divergence from the normal hours of practice. One of the reasons a person may wish to leave is because of sickness or an injury the instructor is not aware of. In such a case the instructor should be warned in order that he or she can make an assessment of the situation and act accordingly.

Noise

There will be no shrieking or shouting during randori and there will be no talking during instruction. The judo signal of submission to an arm-lock or a strangle is a specific tapping action. A shout of submission is not advisable because in a contest, where there may be much noise from the audience, the opponent might not hear it. For the same reason he may not hear a submission made by tapping or banging the mat. If shouting during a randori or training session is allowed, some pupils will never learn the correct method of submission; they will prefer to shout. Judo is a potentially dangerous activity and if pupils are allowed to shout during training the class will not respond when the instructor has to give a sudden command in an emergency. The instructor should be the only person giving commands, and again, if shouting is allowed the main body of the group will not easily recognise the instructor's commands. Similarly, if in a children's class they are allowed to shout or shriek, the instructor will not be able to recognise the genuine shout or scream when a child has been hurt. For all of these reasons a class must be conducted without unnecessary noise. The dojo is after all a place for study and concentration, and it is difficult to concentrate when there is noise going on all around. If spectators are allowed to watch, they should also be advised that they should not talk when the instructor is teaching. There is nothing worse for a coach when he is trying to make an important point than some of his pupils being distracted.

Practising

Judo must not be practised outside the dojo. Judo should only be practised under the watchful eye of a qualified instructor or coach and in the dojo. It is tempting for some people especially children, to show their friends a technique they have studied in the dojo the evening before. It is then when accidents happen, and such accidents are usually due to the uninitiated not knowing how to fall correctly or how to submit in the accepted fashion.

Etiquette

If the aforementioned general dojo rules are observed, there is no reason why everyone in a class should not be able to enjoy their judo. A good all-round club will cater for all groups, from tiny tots to senior citizens, from beginners to high grades – and even for those who just simply want to specialise. Whilst enjoying your judo, it must be seen by these rules that you cannot be too easy-going, flippant or casual. The dojo should be a workshop where you study and work hard on developing the techniques, the skills of judo. The real fun comes from the results of those skills.

Along with the dojo rules there is also a certain etiquette unique to judo and observed by every judoka, not only in the dojo, but at any judo competition. There was a time in Britain when the etiquette was felt to be too alien, and also unnecessary for the sport. It has been seen, however, that the judo etiquette is another attraction and that people do like this aspect. It places a certain dignity and composure upon the sport and helps to create a calm atmosphere on an otherwise energetic and explosive activity. The formal bows which are part of judo etiquette are explained at the beginning of Chapter 5.

4 Fitness

PHYSICAL DEMANDS

Physically, judo is an all-round sport. Because of the training needed to develop the throwing and groundwork techniques, every muscle of the body is utilised. Just look at the range of techniques there are in judo and you will see for yourself. Also, those techniques will depend on speed, strength and stamina if they are to be effective.

Despite there being more leisure time available to most people, and despite sport being projected through the media more than ever before, the average adult is very unfit. This is probably because robot machinery and automation has taken the workload off the backs of the human. Also, it is far too easy these days to jump into a car to travel any small distance. It was recently stated by a Central Council of Physical Education lecturer that only 15 per cent of school-leavers actually continued with or took up a sport after leaving school.

Usually, adults who start judo are, at the very beginning, quite unfit. But the beginner need not worry, judo has a fitness programme built into it. What the beginner must not do during those first few lessons is to overdo things. In seeing the judo skills first demonstrated by an instructor or his assistants, the beginner is usually impressed and will have an immediate appetite to learn those skills. He will tend to throw himself into the study of those skills and their application. This can be dangerous for the unprepared body.

Judo Exercises

In judo there is a system of exercises which, used correctly, can help the beginner to keep pace with his judo training. We call them 'mobility and stretching exercises', and they have traditionally been a part of judo training. The judo coach will always commence a class or training session with such exercises. The beginner will find that in his judo training he is suddenly using muscles he has probably never used before. The sudden demands on the body can cause aches and pains and severe stiffness the day after a training session. A certain stiffness is to be expected, but the aches and pains can be alleviated if the judoka has prepared himself with mobility and stretching exercises. Having reached a certain level of fitness, you must strive to maintain or improve that level. Fitness will only be maintained through regular exercise.

The exercises depicted in *Figs 2* to *13* are standard judo exercises and are designed to 'limber up' preparatory to the actual judo training or randori. Dizziness is quite common with the absolute beginner when he first attempts the tumbling and rolling in judo. In ordinary life, the average adult does not do much tumbling or falling, and when first confronted with the rolling breakfalls or with a groundwork movement he can encounter spells of dizziness. These exercises will soon overcome this problem and will prepare the beginner for the actual judo randori, and help him to gain the equilibrium needed.

The beginner is advised to do just as many exercises as he can comfortably deal with at first. However, when the number of repetitions have become fairly easy, he should increase them and introduce new and more sophisticated exercises.

Exercise One (Fig 2)

The judoka arches his body and, maintaining his balance, stretches backwards. This should be repeated, the second time attempting to stretch further than the first. The judoka then swings his arms forward and, bending at the middle, attempts to lay his forearms on the mat. He repeats this action a second time, again trying to bend further and, if possible, touch the mat with his forehead. The beginner should repeat the overall exercise about ten times.

Fig 2

Exercise Two (Fig 3)

The judoka moves on to the knees and thighs. Try to avoid the temptation to use the hands or finger-tips to keep a balance by placing them on the mat. The judoka squats over onto one leg and attempts to sit on the heel. With the other leg stretched straight he bounces on the heel of the squatting leg twice and then stands up with feet wide apart and swings over to a squatting position on the other leg. This exercise should be repeated five to ten times on each leg.

Fig 3

Exercise Three (Fig 4)

Commonly known as 'cat-dips', this is a very popular judo exercise. It is good for strengthening the arms, back and legs. This exercise illustrates the need for strength, suppleness *and* movement, which is common to judo itself. Start as with the first exercise and then dip the head down, forward and then up, to finish as in *Fig 4b*. Then swing back to the original position. Start with ten to fifteen repetitions, but as this exercise is one that be-

Fig 4a

comes very easy with practice, increase each week by five until you can reach fifty. When the exercise becomes easy to do, try balancing on the finger-tips only. This will increase the strength of the hands, and prepare them for the gripping that will be needed in judo.

Fig 4b

Exercise Four (Fig 5)

Swing the legs over the head, touching the mat with the toes, and then roll forward to touch the toes with the finger-tips. Repeat about fifteen times.

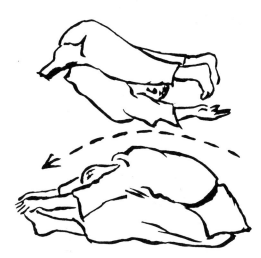

Fig 5

Exercise Five (Fig 6)

This exercise develops suppleness for groundwork. Balancing on both hands face down and with feet apart, swing one leg under the body to rest on the mat as far as you can stretch then, balancing on that foot, swing the other leg under the body to as far as the foot will reach the other side. Repeat five to ten times.

Fig 6

Exercise Six (Fig 7)

'Bunny-hops', commencing from the position shown in *Fig 7*, are very good for developing the legs, which is very important for judo. Hop forward on both feet without rising up, and try to hop the length of the dojo in this position. This exercise can be supplemented with the 'duck walk' by squatting in the same position and walking forward for as far as you can go – but again, remaining in the squat position.

Fig 8

Fig 9

Fig 7

Exercise Seven (Fig 8)

This exercise looks easy, but requires a certain knack in balancing on the buttocks whilst swinging the legs and arms up, for the fingers to touch the toes at 90 degrees. Try this five to ten times.

Exercise Eight (Fig 9)

'Sit-ups' are excellent for developing the stomach muscles, but after getting used to this exercise it becomes easy to cheat by either 'bouncing' the back up off the mat or swinging the arms forward as a counterbalance, making it easier to sit up. There is no point in cheating on yourself, and it certainly will not impress the instructor who has seen all the 'tricks of the trade'. Place the palms of the hands on the back of the head, overlapping if necessary, lie back on the mat and then sit up. It is better if a partner can hold your feet secured to the mat. This is another one of those exercises where, with regular practice, you can attain a high number of repetitions non-stop. The beginner should aim for twenty to start with and, when the exercise becomes easy to do, increase by ten.

Exercise Nine (Fig 10)

This is another exercise which can combat dizziness. Balancing on the back of the head and shoulders, rotate the legs in a 'cycling' motion. Continue for half a minute.

Fig 10

Fig 11

Exercise Ten (Fig 11)

This exercise exemplifies the link between judo exercises and judo skills. The 'bridge 'n twist' is a very good escape move from holds where the opponent is lying on your chest. The beginner should not attempt the overall action immediately, but should first do some simple neck strengthening exercises. For one such exercise simply bridge as in the first illustration and gently roll back and forth on top of the head four or five times. Have a five second rest and then repeat two more times. When the beginner has advanced to the full 'bridge 'n twist', he should practice it on *both sides*.

Exercise Eleven (Fig 12)

This exercise is ideal for developing the strong upper arms needed to effect certain holds. The judoka simply pulls himself along on his forearms the length of the dojo or mat area. Again, it is easy to cheat by using the feet which really should just be allowed to drag. Just as the swimmer will swim a number of lengths of the pool without using a leg action in order to improve the arm-stroke, so a judoka should concentrate on developing the arms for the strong grips he will need to effect his techniques.

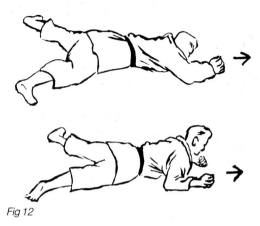

Fig 12

Exercise Twelve (Fig 13)

This exercise is good for both the legs and stomach muscles, and teaches the beginner to 'push off' an opponent correctly without kicking in groundwork. For this purpose, the leg should drive off with the heel just skimming the surface of the mat and, after full extension has been reached, should lift up in a reverse cycling action. The other leg then goes through the same action with repetitions as fast as possible for thirty seconds.

Fig 13

Other Exercises

There are many other such exercises which are used in judo. These exercises should be used preparatory to the actual judo training and should not become the main feature of a judo session. If the beginner feels he needs more exercise, he can do such sequences of exercises outside the normal hours of judo before, after, or between judo classes. In a two-hour judo training session such exercises should take up no more than fifteen minutes at the beginning. The lighter exercises should be reserved for the beginning of a judo training session, and the heavy strength-building exercises at the end.

5 Techniques

FORMAL BOWING

Having run through a series of light exercises the beginner is ready to study specific judo techniques, but first a few words on a certain aspect of judo etiquette, the formal bowing. The beginner will want to feel part of the judo fraternity, and the quickest way to establish this is to become familiar with when, where and how to bow. Do not overdo the bowing; it is not necessary to bow every time you confront another judoka. However, try not to be too casual about it; it is better not to bow at all than to present a floppy and uncoordinated shambles. This shows not only disrespect for the person you are bowing to, but also disrespect for the sport.

On entering or leaving a dojo or mat area, the judoka is expected to bow from a standing position towards the senior instructor, or at least facing the mat. In Japan it is usual to bow to the joseki where the leading judoka and visiting dignitaries sit, but very few dojos outside Japan have a joseki, or if they do, use them to the same ritualistic degree. Similarly, before and after a randori or contest (*shiai*), the judoka will bow simultaneously to his partner or opponent.

Kneeling Bow *(Figs 14 & 15)*

The kneeling bow (*za-rei*) is usually used only for the formal opening and closing of a judo training session or special meeting. In performing the za-rei, avoid raising the hips by remaining seated on the heels, and slide the hands down the top of the thighs to rest, palms down, on the mat just in front of the

knees. Sitting in such a position for some time can be uncomfortable for the average Westerner at first, but with practice he will soon find that he will be able to sit in this fashion for some considerable time.

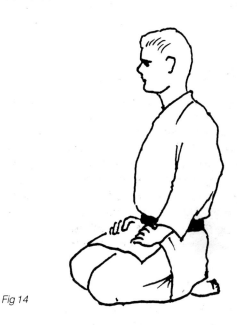

Fig 14

Fig 15

Standing Bow *(Fig 16)*

The standing bow (*tachi-rei*) is performed simply by standing with feet together and bending from the waist, making sure that the head does not flop forward and that a straight line is maintained from the waist to the top of the head. To be absolutely precise, the palms of the hands slide round to the front of the knees and cover the knee caps whilst bending forward. Do not bend too far forward unless you meet royalty or the Emperor of Japan!

THROWING TECHNIQUES

Somewhere in the *gokyo-no-nage-waza* (40 throwing techniques) there is a throw for you, but it is important that the beginner studies each one of them. The instructor cannot tell a beginner which throw is going to be his eventual *tokui-waza,* or favourite match-winning throw. The instructor can, later in the judoka's career, guide and advise on a specific throw which the judoka has found an inclination for. To find the throw that suits you best you have to study all of them. There was a time in the days of non weight-category competitions when an instructor could predict which type of throw would suit you, depending on your build. As competitors are now fairly evenly matched weight for weight, one can no longer speak in terms of 'a small man's throw' or 'a big man's throw'.

In looking at the various throwing techniques I will concentrate first on what I describe as the 'Big Six'. These are the throws that are currently the most popular and statistics from major judo tournaments have shown to be the most widely used and successful. In the course of time fashions and trends change, and so it is with judo. A particular throw becomes popular and largely success-

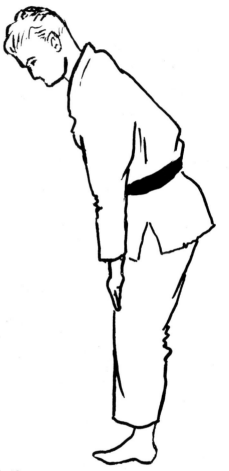

Fig 16

ful, but then other judoka become very aware of that throw and strong defences and counter moves are built up against it. That particular throw then drops out of fashion and another takes its place. But down the years at least one of the 'Big Six' has been in fashion. That is not to say that the other throws should be ignored by any means, as they are often instrumental in leading in to one of t throws.

Note

Before describing each of the judo techniques I should point out that the illustrations depict that point of the technique which identifies it as being a specific technique separate from all others. The illustrations do not show the footwork and arm actions needed for each throw; to do so would require entire volumes of books. Besides, I believe a judoka develops his own style of entry under guidance of the coach. However, as a general guide, *Figs 17* to *21* show the generally accepted entry for one particular throw which is *morote-seoi-age* (both hands shoulder throw).

Fig 19

Fig 20

Fig 17

Fig 18

Fig 21

Fig 22 Tai-otoshi.

Tai-otoshi – body drop (Fig 22)

This is a hand throw and is one of the best for a beginner to learn. In perfecting the throw *Tori* (the thrower) jumps around in front of *Uke* (the person being thrown) to land with feet well apart, and wheels Uke around his own body and over his right foot to 'drop' Uke in front of himself. Compare the illustration with the sequence *(Figs 23* to *25)* showing Neil Adams in action with his tokui-waza. Notice that the power drive by Neil has left him in a good position to follow through to effect a hold down if necessary. This is the mark of a good competitor.

Fig 23 Neil Adams executing a tai-otoshi.

Fig 24 The opponent is now being wheeled round Neil's body.

Fig 25 *Completion of the tai-otoshi. Neil Adams on top of his opponent in full control.*

Morote-seoi-nage — both hands shoulder throw (Fig 26)

This one also is described as a hand throw. If the entry for this throw is perfect Uke can do little to counter the throw and it usually scores *ippon* (maximum ten point score). The illustration depicts a very early stage in the throw *compare this with Figs 27 to 29.* This sequence shows Martin McSorley completing the throw, and again, notice Martin's power drive off the back foot and his ideal position for a hold-down (*osae-komi-waza*) technique.

Fig 26 Morote-seoi-nage.

Fig 27 Martin McSorley demonstrates the
drive-off for the morote-seoi-nage.

Fig 28 Note how Martin is putting himself into
an ideal position for a hold-down.

Fig 29 Completion of the morote-seoi-nage.

Fig 30 Harai-goshi.

Harai-goshi – sweeping loin (Fig 30)

This is one of the most popular of the one-foot throws to the front. Meaning that, whilst supporting his own weight and the weight of Uke on one leg, Tori uses the other leg to sweep his opponent off his feet. The sweeping or 'working' leg should strike Uke across his lower middle and at the top of his thigh. The co-ordination between Tori's pulling (*kuzushi*) and body-positioning (*tsukuri*) needs much study and practice.

ig 31 Uchi-mata.

Uchi-mata – inner thigh (Fig 31)

This is another popular one-foot throw to the front, but this time Tori sweeps the inside of Uke's leg with his 'working' leg with, again, all the weight being supported on his other leg. Now look at the photographic sequence (*Figs 32 to 36*). In *Fig 32* Neil Adams gains entry with his supporting left foot just inside Uke's left foot. *Fig 33* shows 'lift-off' with Uke drop- ping his left arm to encircle Neil's waist in a desperate effort to avert the throw and stop being turned over in the air. *Fig 34* shows the tremendous extension Neil achieves and *Fig 35* demonstrates Neil's total commitment resulting in both he and his opponent being launched into the air. *Fig 36* shows the perfect landing, again with Neil still in complete control.

Techniques

Fig 32 Neil Adams executing the uchi-mata against Eduardo Cerna of Mexico. Notice that Neil has made his entry with his support leg well bent in order to get under the centre of gravity of his opponent. His left foot is ideally placed just inside his opponent's left foot.

Fig 33 Neil's support leg straightens to lift the opponent off the ground.

Fig 34 Support leg at full extension.

Fig 35 The dynamic power generated by Neil lifts his opponent and himself into the air.

Techniques

Fig 36 Neil follows through to devastating effect and scores ippon.

O-soto-gari – major outer reaping (Fig 37)

With this throw Tori does not turn but steps in alongside his opponent, not too deep otherwise he will be easily countered. In stepping in Tori pulls Uke over onto the leg he is going to sweep. He sweeps (or reaps) back, striking the back of Uke's upper right leg with the back of his own upper right leg. In *Fig 38* Robert van de Walle of Belgium is about to score ippon with *o-soto-gari*.

Fig 37 O-soto-gari.

Fig 38 Robert Van De Walle uses his height to score ippon with o-soto-gari.

Fig 39 Tomoe-nage.

Tomoe-nage – stomach throw (Fig 39)

This throw is described as a sacrifice throw because Tori sacrifices his position in order to do it. *Tomoe-nage* is one of the most dramatic of all sacrifice throws. Beginners should be warned that if it does not work, you have left yourself vulnerable to being held down in groundwork. The popular modern variety of *tomoe-nage* is a side stomach throw (*yoko-tomoe-nage*) which lessens the possibility of being caught in groundwork (*ne-waza*) if it is not successful. *Fig 40* shows a *tomoe-nage* in action.

Fig 40 This tomoe-nage scored a waza-ari because the competitor being thrown was able to twist his body in the air, but not sufficiently to completely frustrate the attack.

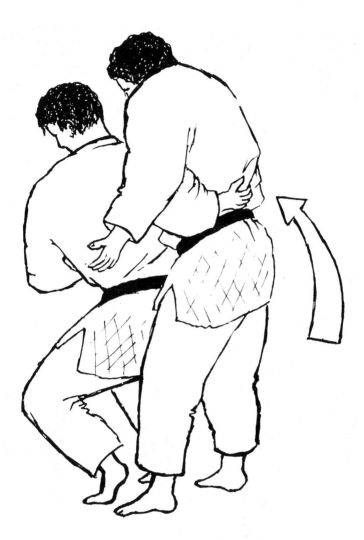

₃ 41 O-goshi.

›-goshi – major hip (Fig 41)

ﬤis is described as a hip throw because the ɔ acts as a car jack in destroying Uke's ﬎lance. Twisting his hip across the oppoᶟnt's front, Tori's right arm wraps round ⲕe's waist. Tori's feet should be placed ᶟ̃ost between Uke's feet and close together with knees well bent. Pulling or locking Uke onto his hip, Tori straightens his legs and at the same time bends forwards, wheeling Uke over onto his back. This is the ideal throw for beginners who are still not sure of their breakfalls because control by Tori can be maintained right to the end.

Fig 42 *Tsuri-goshi.*

Tsuri-goshi — lift-up hip (Fig 42)

Another one of the hip-throw family, but with
this one, as compared to the previous throw
(*O-goshi*), Tori gains purchase on the belt of
Uke and pulls him up onto his hip.

Fig 43 Uki-goshi.

Uki-goshi – floating hip (Fig 43)

With this hip throw there is not the 'jacking-up' action with the hips as with *O-goshi*, nor is there the pulling up action as with *Tsuri-goshi*, but by rotating the shoulders Tori 'floats' Uke on the point of his hip.

Fig 44 Koshi-guruma.

Koshi-guruma – hip wheel (Fig 44)

By holding Uke higher around the neck, Tor
pulls Uke down onto his hip which is turned ir
deep (as with *O-goshi*) and wheels his opponent over the hips.

Fig 45 Seoi-otoshi.

Seoi-otoshi – shoulder drop (Fig 45)

As the name suggests, this is a mixture of *Morote-seoi-nage* and *Tai-otoshi*. It has the hand action of the former and the footwork of the latter. This throw has become very popular in modern-day judo and *Fig 46* shows how Angelo Parisi uses it to such great effect, particularly against taller and heavier opponents.

Fig 46 *Angelo Parisi confounds his opponents by being able to use seoi-otoshi equally well both on the left and on the right.*

Fig 47 Ippon-seoi-nage.

Ippon-seoi-nage – one-arm shoulder throw (Fig 47)

This is another popular and effective technique in the shoulder-throw range. As can be seen, it can be attempted when Tori has been allowed only a one-hand grip on a sleeve. But the correct use of the 'loose' arm is very important. It has to lock high under Uke's armpit. The illustration shows a right-handed *Ippon-seoi-nage,* in which Tori's right bicep should be locked against Uke's right armpit.

Beginners tend to go in too deep with the shoulder which can create a number of problems. As soon as Tori has locked his right arm in and under Uke's armpit, he should pull down across his own stomach with his left hand, ensuring that Uke's right arm is firmly trapped whilst Tori throws him over his right shoulder. If Uke's right arm is not secured firmly, he can slip off or take some avoiding action, frustrating an 'ippon' or maximum score.

Fig 48 Tsurikomi-goshi.

Tsurikomi-goshi – lift-pull hip (Fig 48)

This throw used to be very popular and successful and there is no reason why it should not come back and perhaps join the 'Big Six'.

It is a hip throw using the standard sleeve and lapel grips, but demands deep entry with the hips with Tori's knees well bent.

ig 49 Hane-goshi.

Hane-goshi – spring-hip (Fig 49)

his throw is rarely seen in competition these ays but again, there is no reason why it hould not come back in favour. No doubt it ill but in a more dynamic form. It is one of the ost skilful throws in the *Gokyo*. Tori must achieve tight body contact with his pulling action. With his 'working' leg, in this case the right leg, he creates a platform across Uke's right thigh and with it he 'springs' his opponent off his feet and over.

47

Fig 50 O-guruma.

O-guruma – major wheel (Fig 50)

This one looks very much like *harai-goshi* but in fact is very much different. The 'working' leg does not sweep or reap back as with *harai-goshi*, but remains firmly locked against Uke's right leg just above the knee. There is not the same upper body contact either as with *harai-goshi*; the pulling action must be very powerful, similar to *tai-otoshi*. The person being thrown with *O-guruma* has the feel of being pulled or wheeled over a very low wall which he cannot step over.

51 Hane-makikomi.

ane-makikomi – spring and winding
ig 51)

is is a very powerful throw with a heavy fall
d seems to be the modern alternative to
ne-goshi, possibly because it is less easily
untered. The entry is exactly the same as

with *hane-goshi* but Tori releases his grip on
Uke's lapel, in this case his right hand, and
then uses it to drive Uke's head forward and
down, and continues with a winding action of
his body down to the mat.

Fig 52 Ashi-guruma.

Ashi-guruma – leg wheel (Fig 52)

This throw is usually performed by the very fast and nippy judoka. Performed by an expert you could miss seeing it if you blinked. It is rather like *tai-otoshi* but with one foot n planted on the mat, in this case Tori's rig foot, but sweeping back as a 'working' le and through Uke's lower right leg.

Fig 53 Soto-makikomi.

Soto-makikomi – outer winding (Fig 53)

Another winding throw, but this time Tori laces his right leg across Uke's front and plants his right foot just outside Uke's right foot. At the same time, Tori has released his grip on Uke's left lapel and, driving the back of his right arm against Uke's head, he proceeds to wind down to the mat keeping Uke wrapped firmly to him.

Fig 54 Harai-makikomi.

Harai-makikomi – sweeping and winding (Fig 54)

This is virtually a *harai-goshi,* but instead of sweeping Uke off his feet with the 'working' leg, he lets go (with the right hand in this case), and uses his right arm to force forward and down Uke's head, and spirals down to the mat with a winding action. A *harai-goshi* exponent might convert to this throw when he has found that, though he has locked in deep enough, Uke is still maintaining his balance with a powerful blocking defence.

g 55 O-uchi-gari.

)-uchi-gari – major inner reaping
^ig 55)

would call this a 'light' throw as opposed to
e big 'heavy guns' where overall body action
used. It is, however, a very skilful throw and
iould never be underestimated. I would say
is and the next two throws are 'musts' in the
pertoire of a good judoka. They serve as
peners' or, in some cases, 'finishers' to a
ig throw' attack. In other words they are

ideal in combination attacks. A pure *O-uchi-
gari* depends on good timing. At the right
moment Tori catches with the heel of his
'working' leg (in this case) Uke's left heel, and
sweeps (or reaps) heel first in a semi-circle
action out to the side and back. At the same
time he drives off the back foot, in this case the
left foot, and with a kind of 'bow and arrow'
action with the hands, drives Uke back into
Uke's own left-rear corner.

Fig 56 O-uchi-gake.

O-uchi-gake – major inner hook (Fig 56)

The 'purists' might argue that there is no such throw, and that it is in fact a particular style of *O-uchi-gari*. Videos and slow-motion replays are now used in abundance in judo to analyse the top competitors, and it is a fact that many modern-day competitors are going slightly deeper with the 'working' leg and are 'hooking'. In doing so they are not sweeping the opponent's foot but are remaining hooked i with the 'working' leg, and by a series of hop off the back foot are 'running-off' the oppc nent until he falls down onto his back. In suc a case the arm action also changes, To pushes with both arms driving Uke's hea and shoulders backwards. Such is the evolu tion of judo, and I think it is fascinating an encouraging to see modern-day competitor developing such moves.

g 57 Ko-uchi-gari.

Ko-uchi-gari – minor inner reaping (Fig 57)

In this case, Tori reaches across Uke's front with his right foot and, catching Uke's right heel with the arch of his foot, sweeps Uke's right foot towards his own left foot. At the same time, Tori pushes into Uke's chest with his right forearm, and with his left hand drives Uke's right elbow down.

Fig 58 Kosoto-gari.

Kosoto-gari – minor outer reaping (Fig 58)

Driving Uke's right elbow down into Uke's waist and trying to drive it across Uke's stomach, Tori steps forward with his left foot to place it on the outside of Uke's right foot. Nifty footwork by Tori is required at this stage and, bringing up his right foot he almost replace the left foot by raising his left foot to catc Uke's right heel and sweep Uke's right foo towards the position where Tori was original standing. Tori must make contact with th bottom of his foot on Uke's right heel.

g 59 *Kosoto-gake.*

osoto-gake – minor outer hook
ig 59)

ery similar to the previous throw, after hook-
g his left foot around the back of Uke's right
g, Tori lays his upper body weight into Uke,
driving Uke backwards. Tori can obtain extra
power by hopping and driving off his back or
right foot.

Fig 60 Osoto-guruma.

Osoto-guruma – major outer wheel (Fig 60)

This is a very ambitious technique and, if Tori has not broken Uke's balance to Uke's rear effectively, should not be attempted. If Uke has been able to maintain his balance he can counter this throw. As can be seen, Tori does not attack the nearest leg as with Osoto-ga but reaches right across with his right 'working' leg to sweep both of Uke's legs. Tori ca achieve extra power and drive, forcing Uke head and shoulders back, by releasing his gr on Uke's left lapel and sliding his right arm u and around the left side of Uke's neck.

Fig 61 Yama-arashi.

Yama-arashi – mountain storm (Fig 61)

This is a very dynamic and dramatic throw and is used more often than people realise these days. It is so fast and effective that people often think it is a variation of either *tai-otoshi* or *ashi-guruma*. It is not one of the *Gokyo,* the original 40 throws, but was invented by a small man who became very famous with it. Legend has it that he was so devastatingly effective with it that it was banned for some time. From a normal right posture hold, Tori releases his grip on Uke's left lapel, sliding his right hand across Uke's front, and swiftly seizes Uke's right lower lapel or sleeve. At the same time he spins in, an action requiring very fast footwork, and sweeps Uke's lower right leg. This is not one to practise on beginners as the fall is very heavy.

Fig 62 Morote-gari.

Morote gari – both arms reap (Fig 62)

This is a very popular contest trick rather than a classical throw. Contests are often won with this one in the opening seconds. Tori makes as if to take a high hold on Uke's jacket and then, just as they are about to meet, he drops down, bending both knees, and with both hands scoops Uke's legs from behind. In scooping, Tori achieves more power to the throw by driving his shoulder (in this case the right shoulder) into Uke's stomach.

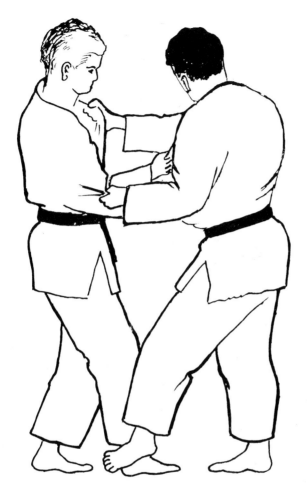

63 De-ashi-barai.

e-ashi-barai – foot dash or sweep ig 63)

metimes known as *De-ashi-harai* which
s the same meaning, this throw is the es-
nce of skill and pure timing. The opportunity
this throw comes when Uke has in some
ay been tricked by Tori to step forward. At
at split second when Uke is about to bear
weight on that foot, Tori catches the out-
de of Uke's advanced foot in a cat's-paw-like
tion with the bottom of his own 'working'
ot, in this case the left foot, and sweeps
ke's advanced foot across the surface of the
mat in front of Uke. Coupled with the foot
sweep on Tori's part, Tori also executes a
sharp unbalancing action with his hands, in
this case lifting and driving across and under
Uke's chin with the right hand, and bearing
down and across Uke's stomach with the left
hand. In modern judo this throw is vastly
underrated by many coaches and competitors and, because of its swift and sudden
application, is often missed or confused with
other throws. The Japanese, in general, still
score very highly with this one in major competition.

Fig 64 Sasae-tsurikomi-ashi.

Sasae-tsurikomi-ashi – propping drawing ankle (Fig 64)

Although a foot throw, there is no sweep with this one. Rather, Tori stops Uke advancing by blocking or 'propping' the advancing foot, and with a powerful lift-pull, draws Uke's up-per body forward and off balance over the fo that has been trapped. Tori can add gre power to his lift-pull by leaning back at angle without bending or 'breaking' in th middle.

Fig 65 Harai-tsurikomi-ashi.

Harai-tsurikomi-ashi – sweeping drawing ankle (Fig 65)

Although it may look very similar to the previous throw, there is a big difference. With this throw Tori sweeps Uke's foot back rather than 'prop' or peg the foot. This means that it works best when Uke is stepping back rather than forward. At the crucial moment, Tori catches the instep of Uke's retreating foot and, with the bottom of his foot placed across Uke's instep, Tori sweeps it further than Uke originally intended to step.

Fig 66 Okuri-ashi-harai.

Okuri-ashi-harai – side-sweeping ankle throw (Fig 66)

The most dramatic and impressive of all the foot throws, because Uke is quite literally swept off both his feet at the same time. The opportunity for this comes when Uke has stepped to the side or is moving to the side, possibly to avoid another kind of attack. Tori steps in close to Uke with his supporting foot, and with the working foot catches Uke on the outside of the foot, and sweeps it into Uke's other foot. With the bottom of his 'working' foot making contact, Tori sweeps both Uke's feet into the air, at the same time checking Uke's upper body weight with a strong pull in the opposite direction.

Fig 67 Hiza-guruma.

Hiza-guruma – knee wheel (Fig 67)

There is no sweep with this throw. Tori steps (in this case) to the outside edge of Uke's left foot with his support foot, and lifts his left 'working' leg to allow the bottom of the foot to catch Uke just below and to the side of Uke's right knee. As with all foot-throws there should

be no kick whatsoever, but a firm placing of the foot to stop Uke stepping forward from the strong pull by Tori with his left hand and lift and drive of the right hand. With the lift-pull Tori should imagine he is driving a truck with a steering wheel of massive circumference and turning, in this case, to his left.

Fig 68 Uki-otoshi.

Uki-otoshi – floating drop (Fig 68)

This is said to be the forerunner of *tai-otoshi* and was also said to be a useful move on the battlefield against adversaries wearing heavy armour. It does still work in modern judo, but usually as a counter move when the opponent is driving his weight forward and onto you. I being pushed or forced back, Tori suddenl drops down at the right moment and, usin his own body weight to pull Uke sharply dowr tips Uke forward and down, wheeling him ove his own forward foot.

ig 69 *Sumi-gaeshi.*

Sumi-gaeshi – corner throw (Fig 69)

Similar to *Tomoe-nage,* this is another sacrifice throw. The major difference being the working' leg, which with this throw catches Jke inside his thigh. In modern judo this one is also being executed to the side so that, if Tori does not score maximum ippon, he can quickly follow through and turn on to Uke by holding him down.

Fig 70 Tani-otoshi.

Tani-otoshi – valley drop (Fig 70)

This is a powerful throw with a very heavy fall and certainly should not be practised on beginners. It is much in evidence in modern-day judo as a counter technique. Tori plants his left foot on the mat just behind Uke's left heel. Notice also how Tori has changed both his grips from the standard grips on Uke's jacket in order to drive Uke's upper body weight backwards.

g 71 Yoko-otoshi.

´oko-otoshi – side drop (Fig 71)

´ith this sacrifice throw, Tori has tipped Uke
￼ his right side and, in order to use his own
ɔdy weight effectively, drives his left leg forward to rest on the mat alongside Uke's right
foot, and throws Uke to the side in the direction of the arrow.

Fig 72 Yoko-wakare.

Yoko-wakare – side separation (Fig 72)

Instead of stepping forward with his left foot as with the previous throw, Tori throws himself down onto the mat by driving his right leg across the front of Uke and hanging his entire body weight onto Uke's jacket. Carried c quickly and expertly at the right moment, To will tip Uke forward and down and wheel hi over his own body.

73 Yoko-gake.

oko-gake – side hook (Fig 73)

though this throw looks like a foot-throw or *hi-waza,* it is classified as a side-sacrifice chnique because Tori goes down to the mat so to land on his side. The beginning of the row is very similar to *Sasae-tsurikomi-ashi* it, using his body weight, Tori hangs on to

Uke and with his left foot catching Uke's right instep, falls backwards and turns to his side at the last moment. Tori must make sure he does not fall to the mat first and will not do so if, at the crucial moment, he turns to his side thus ensuring that Uke falls past him.

Techniques

Fig 74 Uki-waza.

Uki-waza – floating technique (Fig 74)

This sacrifice throw requires absolute skill and the choosing of the right moment to do it. It is best achieved when Uke is defending strongly with his arms and bending forward. Tori throws his left leg out to the left side and along the surface of the mat at the same time dropping under Uke and wheeling him over h own body.

75 Kata-guruma.

ata-guruma – shoulder wheel
ig 75)

his is a very unusual throw and rarely seen
ese days. It does, however, still work as a
urprise' technique and is always worth
udying and keeping in mind for that
pportune moment when the opponent might
uddenly leave himself vulnerable to it. The
ustration depicts the classical style where
ori achieves extended lift by straightening his
gs and wheels Uke from one side, across his
houlders, to the other. The more modern

version is to dive down into a squat position at
right angles to Uke and as close between his
legs as possible, and at the same time drive
the lead arm (the arm nearest to Uke) between
Uke's legs and hook it around Uke's upper
thigh, in this case the thigh of Uke's right leg.
Tori then pulls down sharply with his left hand
stretching Uke across his shoulders – and
then tips Uke sharply over his head.

That concludes the throwing techniques. There are a few others which are very dangerous to practise and cannot be studied from a book. Quite a number of the throws mentioned have more than one style. There is for example, the straight 'working' leg *Uchi-mata* and the bent 'working' leg *Uchi-mata,* and no doubt judo competitors will continue to develop new styles and modify the old ones as time goes by.

GROUNDWORK

Because of the very nature of judo the throws have been shown first. The judo rules dictate that a competitor cannot enter into groundwork unless a throwing technique has been attempted by either one of the competitors. This principle applies throughout and even in randori. You cannot simply fall down and pull your opponent down into groundwork either. However, this does not mean to say that the throwing techniques and the groundwork techniques have to be studied separately. Once having gained a working understanding of at least one throw it is good for the beginner to then study groundwork moves, particularly those that may lead easily from the throw.

Holding Techniques

We now come to the *ne-waza* (ground techniques) and commence with the *osae-waza* or holding techniques. To achieve maximum score with a holding technique it must be maintained for at least thirty seconds. The judoka therefore has to train himself not only to secure the hold correctly, but to maintain it for a period of time despite any efforts the opponent might make to escape from it. There are lesser scores for hold-downs depending on the length of time the hold has been maintained inside the thirty second maxi-

mum, but you should endeavour to develop hold strong enough to keep the oppone pinned on his back and immobilised for indefinite period of time. You should tra yourself to secure such a powerful hold tha cannot be broken, and from which there is escape. That takes a lot of training and pra tice.

As has been pointed out earlier in this boc though it is important to study all the throw we each develop our own *tokui-waza* favourite techniques. These become our ov special throwing techniques, the ones v have the most success with. Very few peor develop more than three or four of su throws. Even a world class competitor v only employ those four or five 'reliable against his own kind. In groundwork, hov ever, the approach is much different. A go effective judoka must study every *ne-wa* technique that there is and learn as much he can about groundwork tactics. A pers who is good at *nage-waza* but weak in r waza soon becomes known and others v by various tricks, exploit this weakness. Als in *tachi-waza* a judoka can more often th not select the throw he wants to use, where in groundwork the judoka cannot select easily and must use the technique which c cumstances and his opponent have pr sented the opportunity for him to do. Yc knowledge of groundwork must therefore much greater.

Hon-kesa-gatame – basic scarf ho (Fig 76)

This hold is the most widely used and usually the first beginners are taught. It is o of the easiest to slide into following a throw attack. If you are bigger than your oppone ou can afford to use your weight and lie across the chest, but the best method and certainly the one which should be used if you are lighter than your opponent, is the one where Tori lays his head forward and down, as close to the mat as possible, as in the illustration. Tori's head is turned slightly to his left and it is important to sit on the mat alongside Uke with legs spread to create a good firm base. Tori should ensure that Uke's right arm is trapped by locking his forearm with the inside of his own left bicep and holding Uke's upper right sleeve securely with his own left hand. Tori's right arm encircles Uke's neck and his right hand grips Uke's upper right collar.

In practising and developing a good strong hold the judoka should first take note of all the points made, and once satisfied that it is fairly well applied, should then get his partner to struggle and try to escape in order to test it. In applying what they think is a strong hold most beginners tend to stiffen and make rigid every muscle in their body. This is a mistake, for the experienced judoka will use that rigidness to make his escape. It takes much practice and study to develop a good strong hold whilst at the same time conserving all your energy.

It is also always a good maxim to practise every hold on *both sides* of the partner. Whatever side of the opponent you may find yourself – *you must go for the nearest hold available.*

g 76 *Hon-kesa-gatame.*

Fig 77 Kuzure-kesa-gatame.

Kuzure-kesa-gatame – broken scarf hold (Fig 77)

The word 'broken' in this context does not by any means suggest that this hold is weaker than the previous one; it merely means that it is just another form of the same family of holds and slightly different from the 'basic' technique. At first, beginners will find that this hold is not so easy to maintain against a struggling opponent as the previous hold, but with practice it can in time become even stronger. Instead of encircling Uke's neck with his right arm as with the previous hold, Tori drives his right arm between Uke's upper left arm and trunk, and with his right hand grips Uke's

jacket at the shoulder. This hand is then read to act as a 'prop' palm down on the ma should Uke suddenly try to bridge to his lef

Ushiro-kesa-gatame – reverse sca hold (Fig 78)

People tend to give up on this one far to quickly. At first it does seem to be weaker tha the previous holds, but with practice on in creasingly stronger partners, it can becom very powerful. Tori's left hand has passe under Uke's left shoulder and is grippin Uke's belt.

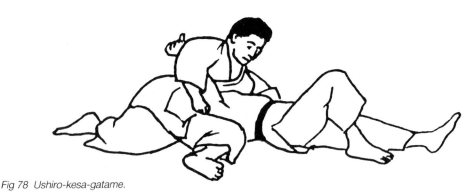

Fig 78 Ushiro-kesa-gatame.

Fig 79 Makura-kesa-gatame.

Makura-kesa-gatame – pillow scarf hold (Fig 79)

This technique virtually explains itself. By making a 'pillow' with the upper part of his left leg, Tori ensures that Uke cannot bridge, and achieves a 'wrap-round' effect by gripping his own hands together.

Mune-gatame – chest hold (Fig 80)

This hold is achieved by Tori reaching across Uke with his left arm and at the same time driving Uke's left arm up towards Uke's head and tucking his own head under that arm, and then reaching down with his left hand to grip Uke's belt. Tori can make this hold either crouched over his opponent on his knees with knees wide apart and against the opponent, or lying as flat as possible with legs outstretched flat on the mat.

Fig 80 Mune-gatame.

Fig 81 Kata-gatame.

Kata-gatame – shoulder hold (Fig 81)

Not only is this a good hold, but with sufficient pressure on the neck it can result in a submission from a strangle. Note that Tori's right leg is outstretched creating a 'prop'. His left leg is crouched up underneath himself and wedged against Uke's body. It is rarely possible to 'bridge 'n twist' against this hold and usually the only way out is to roll the legs, in this case, over the right shoulder.

Hon-kami-shiho-gatame – basic upper four quarters hold (Fig 82)

The opportunity for this hold usually com▮ when Tori has attacked with a sacrifice thro and, not having been entirely successful w▮ the throw, quickly turns to pin Uke's che▮ with his own chest, and with his arms passir under Uke's shoulders, seizes Uke's belt each side of his waist. Beginners tend to too far down on Uke's chest and therefo make it easy for an experienced judoka quickly 'bridge 'n twist' out of the hold. Bigg▮ and stronger judoka usually prefer a differe▮ style where they are crouched over with kne▮ drawn up.

Fig 82 Hon-kami-shiho-gatame.

Fig 83 *Kuzure-kami-shiho-gatame.*

Kuzure-kami-shiho-gatame – broken upper four quarters hold (Fig 83)

This is very similar to the previous hold, but instead of both hands gripping Uke's belt, one (in this case Tori's left) has passed under Uke's left armpit and is gripping Uke's collar with fingers inside at the back of his neck. Both with this hold and the previous hold Tori should always ensure that his body is lying in line with Uke's body. If, in his struggles to escape, Uke can manoeuvre his body so that it lies at right angles to Tori, he can make a powerful 'bridge 'n twist' and escape.

It is especially important for beginners to note that for this type of hold where Tori is lying face down, his toes are curled under. There are two important reasons for this, one is in order that he does not suffer mat-burns on the instep with the sudden movement and friction that can occur, and the other is that by so placing his toes he has the ability to move his legs faster when reacting to the threat of Uke escaping.

Hon-tate-shiho-gatame – basic vertical four quarters hold (Fig 84)

Sometimes referred to as the 'straddle-hold', Tori in fact straddles Uke with his legs and, locking his knees in against Uke's body, locks one of Uke's arms against Uke's head. Tori can grip his own hands to effect an encircling hold with his arms, or he can encircle Uke's neck with one arm and grip his own jacket leaving the other arm free to act as a 'prop' should Uke suddenly try to bridge.

Fig 84 *Hon-tate-shiho-gatame.*

Techniques

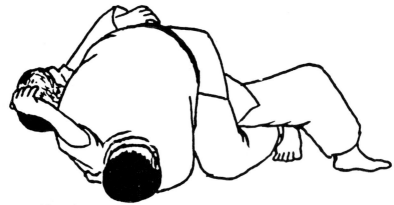

Fig 85 Kuzure-tate-shiho-gatame.

Kuzure-tate-shiho-gatame – broken vertical four quarters hold (Fig 85)

This is a variation on the previous hold with Tori trapping and securing one arm and shoulder rather than the head of Uke also. In this illustration Tori's right hand would be gripping Uke's belt at the back. With both these holds Tori can lock his heels in under Uke's thighs for greater control if he has the length of leg and is able to do it. He should however be careful not to straighten his legs on Uke's legs as this could constitute a leg-lock, which in a contest would be illegal.

Hon-yoko-shiho-gatame – basic side four quarters hold (Fig 86)

There are a number of styles or variations to this hold. If Tori has sufficient span, he holds Uke's belt, in this example with his right hand, and with his left hand passing at the back of Uke's neck, grips high on Uke's left lapel. The beginner should experiment with the various leg positions to see which one suits him best. Tori can lie flat on his stomach with legs astride, or with one knee wedged against Uke, or crouched with both knees against Uke.

Fig 86 Hon-yoko-shiho-gatame.

Kuzure-yoko-shiho-gatame – broken side four quarters hold (Fig 87)

This hold would be more suited to the smaller person than the previous one. Because Tori does not have the arm span to reach right round to Uke's belt or tails of the jacket, he holds the seat of Uke's trousers with his right hand. If Tori keeps his right arm straight it will have the effect of pinning Uke to the mat by the seat of his pants. Tori, however, should keep his head high up on Uke's chest and not allow Uke to push it down to his waist, otherwise Uke will be able to sit up and escape.

Fig 87 Kuzure-yoko-shiho-gatame.

Strangle Techniques

We now look at the *shime-waza* or strangle techniques. Those attempted from behind are likely to be the most successful as the opponent can see what is going on with strangles from the front, and if he is experienced can frustrate the attempt. But there are occasions when, if they have been applied swiftly and very skilfully, they will work. Beginners should not attempt *shime-waza* or *kansetsu-waza* (arm-locks) on each other until they have had good grounding and experience practising the submission signals. On being given such a signal Tori *should immediately relax the pressure.*

Techniques

Nami-juji-jime – normal cross strangle (Fig 88)

Reaching as high as possible on Uke's lapels, and with thumbs inside the jacket and forearms crossed, Tori pulls Uke towards himself with a firm scissor-like action until Uke submits with two sharp taps anywhere on Tori's body.

Gyaku-juji-jime – reverse cross strangle (Fig 89)

Very much the same as the previous technique but this time with fingers inside the jacket.

Kata-juji-jime – half cross strangle (Fig 90)

Similar to the two previous techniques but in this case thumb inside the jacket on one side and fingers inside the jacket on the other side.

Fig 89 Gyaku-juji-jime.

Fig 88 Nami-juji-jime.

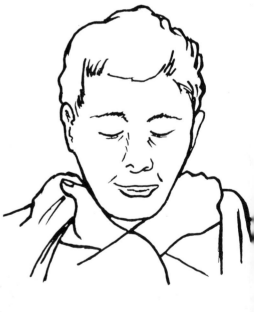

Fig 90 Kata-juji-jime.

Tsuki-komi-jime – thrusting strangle (Fig 91)

Holding both lapels, Tori thrusts across Uke's throat with one hand, with the lapel edge against Uke's throat, and pulls towards himself on the other lapel.

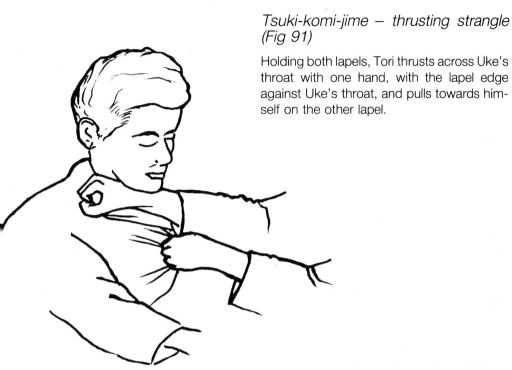

Fig 91 Tsuki-komi-jime.

Morote-jime – both hands strangle (Fig 92)

This is one of those sudden surprise 'trick' strangles which should never be underestimated. Even experienced competitors have been caught out because of its sudden application and immediate effectiveness. Holding high on Uke's lapels with thumbs inside, Tori rolls his clenched fists upwards until the thumbs appear, and with his knuckles maintains the pressure on the neck until Uke submits.

Fig 92 Morote-jime.

Techniques

Hadaka-jime – naked strangle (Fig 93)

This is called the naked strangle because this technique can be applied without using the jacket. Tori slides one hand across the throat of Uke and, resting it in the other upturned hand, pulls back towards himself placing pressure on the throat with the thumb side of the wrist. The experienced judoka will bury his chin into his chest as soon as he suspects his opponent is going to attempt a rear strangle, in which case Tori should bore his way in with his knuckles from the side and under the chin, in this case with his right hand.

Fig 93 Hadaka-jime.

Okuri-eri-jime – sliding lapel strangle (Fig 94)

Good preparation is needed for this strangle. Sliding his left hand between Uke's left arm and trunk, Tori grips Uke's left lapel stretching it downwards. At the same time his right arm passes across Uke's right shoulder and across his chest to grip high on Uke's left lapel, thumb inside the lapel. Having done its job in making access easier for Tori's right thumb, Tori's left hand releases Uke's left lapel and passes across the front of Uke's chest to grip high on Uke's right lapel, again with thumb inside. Tori then straightens his arms forward and the strangle immediately takes effect. In effecting the actual strangle, beginners tend to want to pull with both arms elbows outwards, but this is using brute strength and many experienced *judoka* have powerful necks strong enough to withstand such pressure. Greater effect can be achieved with this type of *okuri-eri-jime* by straightening the arms. However, there are other sliding-lapel strangles which require a different application.

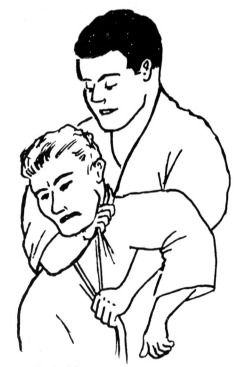

Fig 94 Okuri-eri-jime.

Kata-ha-jime – single wing strangle (Fig 95)

The preparation for this technique is the same as with the previous technique, but instead of passing his left hand across the chest of Uke to grip high on Uke's right lapel, Tori drives his left arm deep and high behind Uke's neck.

Sode-guruma-jime – sleeve wheel strangle (Fig 96)

Personally, I would describe this technique as eri-guruma-jime which means lapel wheel strangle. With his left hand passing across the front of Uke, Tori seizes Uke's right lapel, pulling it across and up until he can transfer the lapel into his right hand. On letting go with his left hand, Tori passes it behind Uke's neck and grips the material of the jacket on Uke's right shoulder.

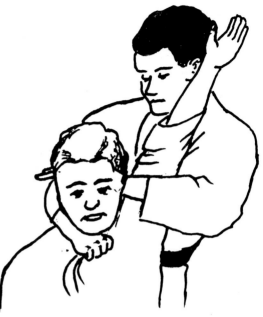

Fig 95 *Kata-ha-jime.*

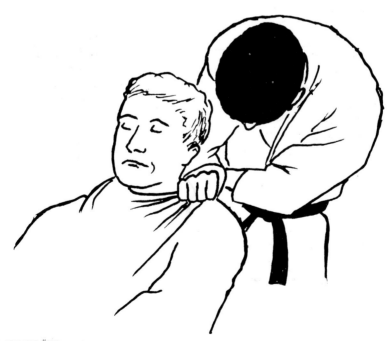

Fig 96 *Sode-guruma-jime.*

Techniques

Koshi-jime – hip strangle (Fig 97)

With Uke on all fours (as in the case shown in the illustration) Tori, whilst kneeling on his right knee alongside Uke, thrusts his left hand under Uke's chin to grip high on Uke's right lapel, and then, pulling the lapel across Uke['s] throat, drives his right leg and hip forward[.] Resting his right hip on Uke's left shoulder T[o] is able to exert greater control and pressur[e]

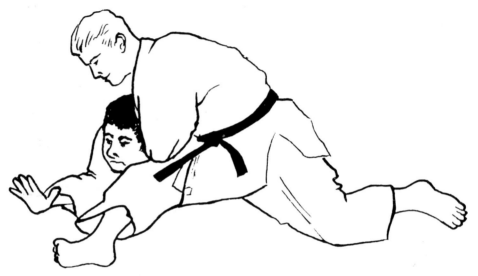

Fig 97 Koshi-jime.

Arm-locks

The only arm-locks that are allowed in judo competition under the Contest Rules are those where pressure is applied to the elbow joint only. This is because shoulder locks and wrist-locks cannot so easily be controlled in the flurry and excitement of a hard-fought contest. Such techniques, however, do appear in some of the judo *kata,* and in particular in the *go-shin-jutsu.* These techniques would only be taught to responsible students of reasonably high grades.

Ude-gatame – straight arm-lock (Fig 98)

For convenience, the illustration depicts th[e] arm-lock being attempted in a certain positio[n] where it can be seen clearly. However, invar[i]ably the arm-lock is attempted in situation[s] where the body of either Tori or Uke block[s] from view the actual technique. Such situa[-]tions demand very capable and experience[d] referees. Notice that the pressure is place[d] slightly above the elbow and that Tori is usin[g] his chin and neck to control the arm in ord[er] that Uke cannot wriggle out of the trap. T[ori] should ease on the pressure firmly and shou[ld] not suddenly snatch or jerk the arm.

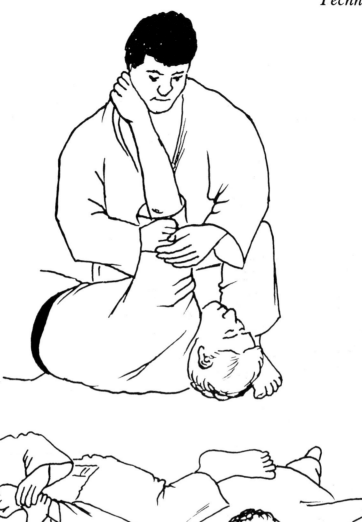

98 Ude-gatame.

99 Hiza-gatame.

Hiza-gatame – knee arm-lock (Fig 99)

Assume that Uke is trying to obtain a hold or is trying to strangle Tori, and is in a dominant position bending over Tori. Tori seizes the wrist of an outstretched arm and slides swiftly to that side and onto his side, swinging his knee (in this case the left knee) up and onto the elbow of Uke's outstretched arm. *Ashi-gatame* is very similar, but with Tori wedging the foot of the leg that is putting pressure on Uke's arm, under Uke's chin.

Techniques

Fig 100 Ude-garami.

Ude-garami – arm entanglement (Fig 100)

Sometimes referred to as 'figure-four arm-lock', Tori is on his knees or stomach face down and reaches across Uke's chest for the furthest arm. In this case he would first seize the wrist with his right hand and then loop his left arm under the upper right arm of Uke and then grip his own right wrist. Tori exerts pressure by pinning Uke's right arm to the mat and slowly driving Uke's right elbow towards Uke's feet, making sure that Uke does not straighten his arm. If Uke does straighten his arm Tori can convert the technique into a straight arm-lock, but this would take practice to perfect.

Juji-gatame – cross straight arm-lock (Fig 101)

There are many good opportunities of approaches for this technique, and in major tournaments it is one of the highest ground-work scorers these days. The approach can be made either from a throwing attack or rolling the opponent in groundwork, and good judoka will study as many ways as possible. Assuming in this case that Tori has attacked with tai-otoshi and has scored less than ippon. Tori maintains his hold on Uke's right sleeve and, stepping across Uke's neck, sits down as close as possible to Uke, making sure he keeps Uke's right arm straight with the thumb of that arm pointing upwards. Tori then exerts pressure by raising his hips slowly and at the same time pulling Uke's right hand down to his chest.

Fig 101 Juji-gatame.

102 Waki-gatame.

Waki-gatame – armpit hold (Fig 102)

This is a very dangerous arm-lock and should be practised with care. Tori should make sure that pressure is being placed on the elbow joint and not on the shoulder.

Ao-muku-yoko-shiho-gatame – facing upwards side four quarters (Fig 103)

This and the following technique are rarely seen in magazines or books, but they are included here because they have become very common in recent years, especially at junior competitions. The illustration speaks for itself.

103 Ao-muku-yoko-shiho-gatame.

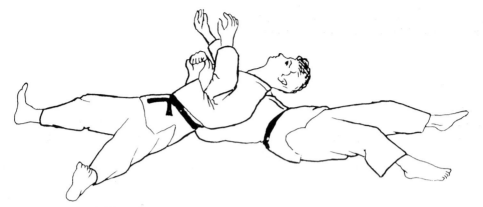

Fig 104 Ao-muku-kami-shiho-gatame.

Ao-muku-kami-shiho-gatame – facing upwards upper four quarters (Fig 104)

This technique usually results from a rolling action when both competitors have been on all fours. Locking his hands under Uke's armpits, Tori has rolled completely over taking Uke with him and then, gripping his hands in 'monkey-grip' or 'sailor's grip', arches back maintain the hold and keep Uke pinned on h back.

6 Competition

Because of the very nature of judo, every judoka has the competitive instinct. Since judo became an Olympic sport, however, a marked 'competitor' element has developed. There is some kind of judo tournament taking place somewhere in the United Kingdom almost every weekend of the year. It is also a fact that judo is a participation sport. By that I mean that the average judo enthusiast is not content to just watch other people doing judo, but is involved some way or another.

When and at what stage of learning judo the 'contest' interest takes a hold varies from person to person. Some start out right from the beginning wanting to enter contests. Others find that through the grading contests they like the competition aspect. Still others are fired with enthusiasm when, after seemingly endless practice and training, a technique suddenly works. I have pointed out earlier in this book how success with a technique can change a person.

CONTEST AREA *(Fig 105)*

Just as a footballer must be familiar with the markings and distances of a football pitch, so the judo competitor must know the judo contest area. In a contest the judo competitor has to employ tactics designed to trick his opponent into making a mistake, but he also uses tactics making full use of and sometimes exploiting the contest area. The standard measurement of one piece of judo mat is two metres by one metre and the contest area is made up of these pieces. The area surrounding the inner box is known as the 'danger area'

and the mats used are coloured red. All the other mats are coloured green.

The red area is part of the contest area and is a 'warning zone', telling the competitor that if he voluntarily steps over the outside edge into the outside 'safety area' he will incur a penalty. It is seen as running away from the fight. In the illustration the outside 'safety area' is two metres wide all round which is the minimum width for domestic events in Britain, but the width required for international tournaments is 2.5 metres. As mats are not manufactured to half metre widths, the organisers of such an event would have to lay a 'safety area' three metres wide.

The international competition area should be a minimum of 14m x 14m and a maximum of 16m x 16m. This includes the inner box of green mats, the square of red mats comprising the danger area and the outside safety area of green mats.

The 'safety area' is so called because one or both competitors can career out and over the outside edge of the danger area in a flurry of activity. Also, a competitor can still be thrown out into the safety area provided the thrower has not stepped over the outside edge of the danger area and into the safety area to do so. For this, and in the case of a sacrifice throw when more than half of the body has landed in the safety area before his opponent has actually been thrown, the attacker can incur a penalty. In avoiding a throw a competitor can step out and not be penalised, and in fact the thrower can step out or land in the safety area, provided he does so after the person being thrown has landed in the safety area first. Action in a judo contest

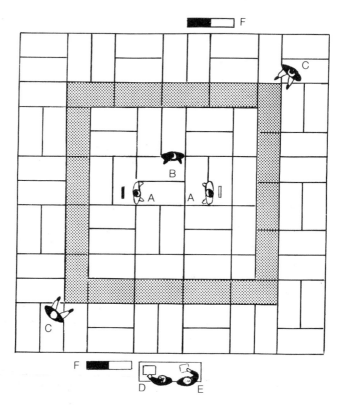

Fig 105 Layout of a contest area. A competitors; B referee; C line judges; D time-keeper; E recorder; F electronic score-boards (manual flip-over score-boards may be used).

can be very complicated and fast, and the referee therefore has to be highly competent in recognising moves as being valid or invalid, particularly when they occur in the danger area. For this reason and because everything that occurs cannot always be seen from one vantage point, the referee is assisted by two line-judges who themselves should be qualified referees. They are seated at two corners diagonally opposite each other in the safety area, and indicate to the referee their judgement paying particular attention to any action taking place in or near the danger area. It should be pointed out that a competitor can incur a penalty for deliberately pushing his opponent over the outside edge of the danger area without attempting any genuine judo technique. As with any sportsman or sports-

woman, a judo competitor can become quite an actor and only an experienced referee will recognise that which is a genuine effort.

Method of Competition

The method of competition varies depending on the level of tournament, but usually they are of the 'knock-out and repechage' variety. This means the winners proceed to the final and the losers to those finalists contest the two bronze medals in the repechage. Methods may also vary slightly from country to country and with tournaments within a country. National events organised by the British Judo Association consist of first round pools in which three, four or five competitors fight each other. Those coming first and second in the ol will then proceed to the first round knock-t contests. Most countries use this method. In registering the results on the competition ms the recorder will use a legend. The andard legend used by British Judo Assoition recorders is shown below.

owing Procedures

dhesive red and white tapes 25 centimetres ng should be fixed to the mat and set four etres apart from the very centre of the const area and parallel to the timekeeper and corder's table. These red and white tapes nould correspond to the side the scorebards are marked (red is always to the right the referee when he is standing at the 'start' osition). The first competitor called to the ontest area (wearing the red 'contest' belt) nould take up his or her position on the red dhesive red tape) marker, 'toeing the line' so speak. The other competitor will be wearing e white 'contest' belt and will stand at the hite marker. When both competitors are anding at their markers they bow to each ther – and *not* to the referee. They then take

one step forward simultaneously and wait for the referee's command of *hajime* which signals the start of the contest. When the referee makes this call the competitors *do not* bow again but immediately 'join in battle'.

When the referee calls *sore-made* to end the contest, both competitors should position themselves one pace in front of the appropriate marker (adhesive red or white tape). When the referee is satisfied that there is a clear result he will take one step forward and indicate the winner. If there is no score or the scores are even, the referee will call *hantei* and two seconds later will raise his right arm straight above his head, fingers stretched upward with the palm of the hand inwards – and at the same time the judges will raise their red or white flag indicating the competitor they each consider to be the winner (i.e. the competitor who was the more dominant, attacked the most, and so on). If the judges are in agreement and the referee is of the same opinion, he will indicate the winner in accordance with their collective opinion. If, however, his opinion differs from that of the two judges he can delay giving the decision in order to

LEGEND		Points Value
Ⓣ	Ippon as a result of a throw	10
Ⓗ	Ippon as a result of a hold	10
Ⓒ	Ippon as a result of a choke (strangle)	10
Ⓛ	Ippon as a result of a lock (elbow lock)	10
T	Waza-ari throw	7
H	Waza-ari hold	7
S	Win by superiority	5, 3 or 1
Ⓐ	Win as a result of a penalty against opponent	7, 5 or 3
SG	Win by sogo-gachi (compound win)	10
HM	Win by hansoku-make (disqualification)	10
FG	Win by fusen-gachi (default non-appearance of opponent)	10
KG	Win by kiken-gachi (withdrawal of opponent during contest)	10
D	Drawn contest (used in team competitions only)	0
L	Loss	0

discuss with them their reasons. He will then once again call *hantei* and must give the decision based upon the majority verdict. In a team tournament when there are no scores or the scores are equal, the judges will raise both red and white flags at the call of *hantei* to indicate a draw. Once the referee has left the contest area it will not be possible to change the decision.

Officials

Of the three officials controlling the course of the contest, the referee gives the commands and indicates the scores or penalties when he deems they are warranted. A judge can intervene if he does not agree with the referee's decision, in which case the referee must then consult the other judge. He can abide by his decision if the other judge does not disagree with it, but if both judges disagree he must amend his decision to that agreed by the two judges and indicate accordingly. The other

two important officials who monitor the co test are the timekeeper and recorder.

For purposes of identification one of t competitors wears a red belt (usually the fir to be called by the announcer) and the othe white belt. If the contest runs to the allotte time (usually five minutes for senior men, fo minutes for senior women and three minute for juniors) without any score whatsoever, th referee will call for the judges to give the opinion as to which competitor they felt wa the more dominant.

Signals (Figs 106 to 110)

Figs 106 to *110* show the signals the refere uses to indicate the scores. In giving suc signals the referee will also call out the score but for the hard of hearing or if the audienc should be particularly noisy such signals a invaluable when following the progress of contest or tournament. They and their inte pretation are therefore worth studying.

Fig 106 *Ippon — maximum ten point score terminating the contest.*

Fig 107 *Waza-ari awasete ippon — a seven point score added to a previous waza-ari scored by the same competitor, resulting in the maximum ten points win and terminating the contest.*

Fig 108 Waza-ari — a seven point score.

Fig 109 Yuko — a five point score.

Fig 110 Koka — a three point score.

TRAINING FOR COMPETITION

Because there are judo competitions for all levels and all ages these days there is a tendency to concentrate more on fitness training than working on skills. For the long-term competitor this is a mistake. The popular champions, and those who are really impress-ive, are those who have a range of skilful techniques. It takes on average nine years for a competitor to get from beginner stage to international class and, sadly, many competi-tors are in too much of a hurry and want to cut corners if they can. There is really no substi-tute for hard work and constant application to skill training, and there are no short cuts. Having said that, however, the competitor can improve his training and take much of the monotony out of it.

I cannot emphasise too often the need for skill training at an early stage. I have heard a number of British team managers complain that some of the judoka who have fought their way into a national squad have not studied sufficient technique, and having fought their way into a national squad are unable to learn new skills once they have arrived there. This is because at that level they cannot risk ex-perimenting with new techniques and are by that time too set in their ways.

The influx of junior competition over the last ten years, particularly in Britain, has meant that young competitors and their coaches have had more of an eye on short-term re-sults. This, coupled with the introduction of the lower scores of *yuko* and *koka,* has meant young competitors have been content to win with limited skills and low scores. Such young competitors, having experienced success, find the transition to senior judo very difficult and it is usually at this stage that they give up. It is interesting to note, and junior competition has been in vogue for sufficient time now to make comparisons, that very rarely has a junior national champion been able to reach the same level as a senior.

Assuming the competitor has given suffi-cient consideration to all of the techniques illustrated in this book, and by now has be-come reasonably proficient at some of them (and continues to work at them), let us now look at the more advanced judo approach.

Fig 111 Alexandra Schreiber of West Germany throws Roswitha Hartl of Austria cleanly to the mat with an uchi-mata.

Fig 112 Alexandra maintains control throughout the throw.

113 Alexandra lands on top of her opponent, well in control.

ADVANCED JUDO

he use of combination techniques (*ren-raku-
aza*) is an important aspect of competition
do. A beginner can be thrown by a higher
ade easily with single-technique attacks,
ut as a judoka progresses up the grade
dder he becomes more aware and is not so
asily caught by such direct approaches. It is
that stage that the judo competitor must
crease his repertoire by way of combination
continuation techniques (*ren-zoku-waza*).
here are many such recognised combina-
ons but one does not necessarily have to
onform to these, and a competitor can cre-
e or indeed invent his own. The principle of a
ombination is simply that Tori attacks with
he particular technique in a certain direction
Uke defends — and then Tori changes to
other technique in the opposite direction. It
assumed that in defending against an attack
one direction, Uke will be weak in the oppo-
e direction, and this is often the case.

People learn, however, and in time and at a
higher level of competition, direct opposites
will no longer always work. It is then that the
competitor must work out combinations at
varying angles and even, at times, in the same
direction as the original attack. Having worked
on one particular combination, it is then good
to work at it vice versa. For example when the
judoka has perfected *seoi-nage* into *o-uchi-
gari*, then he should work on *o-uchi-gari* into
seoi-nage. Provided the competitor keeps an
active and open mind, there is no limit to the
combinations he can create for himself. I
should point out that the initial attack should
not be treated as a 'feint', as in boxing. A
boxer has to react to what he sees, but an
experienced judoka reacts to what he feels —
and if the original attack is not sufficiently
strong as to pose a threat, he will not react.

Having built up his *tokui-waza*, a good
competitor will not only link it with another
technique to form a combination, but will also
improve on it to suit different circumstances.

Fig 114 Neil Adams using uchi-mata on Johan Van Heest of Holland in the preliminaries of the 1983 British Open Championships.

Sometimes, when the initial attack has not achieved its aim, it is good to continue with the same technique, to press home the attack. There is always the danger of being countered when applying such tactics but again, a good competitor will train himself to be aware of such dangers. Having blocked or in some other way defended against an initial attack, some people relax their guard just for a mo-ment. This is the ideal moment for anoth-er attack – or continuing with the same tec-nique. Very often the same technique or a attack in the same quarter is not expected

There are also some throwing techniqu-which can be pressed home to the end. W-*osoto-gari* for example, Tori can contin-

Fig 115 Neil's power has lifted both competitors off the ground.

hopping on the support leg in the direction of the throw. It is easier to hop forward on one leg than hop back, and in using such tactics a good competitor should be prepared to hop the width of the contest area. In being forced to hop backwards, Uke's stance will gradually weaken and sudden success is often achieved by pressing home such an attack.

One often sees such opportunities missed either because the attacker has not realised that his opponent is at the end of his tether, or he himself has not had the stamina to maintain such an attack. Judo training builds up stamina, but the competitor must strive constantly to improve his own stamina to match the level of competition he is entering.

Fig 116 The completion of the throw, for which Neil scores ippon.

In building up stamina *uchi-komi* plays a great part. There has been much discussion about the values and the weaknesses of *uchi-komi*. *Uchi-komi* is the traditional method of learning a throw. The principle behind it is that if a particular movement is practised many thousands of times it will eventually become a natural skill. It is no good a competitor having to think about his throw in a contest, it should be part of him, to be used when the right moment presents itself.

Uchi-komi is practising a throw without throwing, and therein lies the weakness. The ideal would be to practise the complete throw many times over, but there are very few partners prepared to put up with such continuous eatment, particularly if it is a heavy or winding row. In recent years the crash mat has become standard dojo equipment and it is ost valuable for teaching total commitment a throwing technique. *Uchi-komi* still has important part to play – but only if used orrectly.

When a certain throwing technique has become familiar to a judoka there is then a ndency for that judoka to treat *uchi-komi* on at particular technique as a kind of ritual. at is a mistake and it is then when *uchi-komi* ecomes useless. *Uchi-komi* should be kept ve' and should be practised on the move, ot static. In my opinion it is most important to ave a good *uchi-komi* partner. If he is imginative, he will react as he would in competion and also point out your weaknesses. nowing your limitations he will defend accordingly but not make it impossible for you. A holly defensive partner, or one who does not spond in any way is absolutely useless to ou.

There are times when a good *uchi-komi* artner is not available, or all you want to do is nprove your pulling power for a throw. In uch situations a good 'training trick' is the se of rubber tyre inner tubes. Cut according-, these can be fixed to the dojo wall or to a ost and then the judoka can practise his ulling power as in *Fig 117*. Obviously, there re only certain throws for which this aid has ny value, but such throws are among the

Fig 117 You can practise your pulling power using rubber tyre inner tubes.

popular ones. It is most important to ensure that the inner tube rubber is fixed securely and that it is checked every so often. With much use they can weaken or the rubber can perish.

7 The Judo Instructor

'Judo instructor' was, many years ago, the general term used to describe a person teaching judo. These days the term 'judo coach' is in common use. The word 'coach' can suggest that such a person is more concerned with teaching tactics of play rather than teaching specific skills. As this book is concerned with skills I would therefore prefer to use the word 'instructor'. Having said that, I would not wish to get involved in a long discourse as to what people might feel are the differences. In the interests of progress they are, in my opinion, one and the same. I have seen all kinds of people teaching judo and whether they call themselves 'instructors' or 'coaches' does not really matter. It is their experience or qualifications or both which have placed them in that position. A club committee will, in the best interests of their club, appoint the best person they can find to teach at that club. A sports centre manager or a local authority will, because they themselves do not have any kind of judo background, consider the qualifications of applicants they may wish to employ. By and large the standard of judo coaches and instructors in the British Judo Association is very good. This is because, being the official governing body in the United Kingdom for judo, it has a responsibility to produce qualified people of good standard. I would therefore stress to the reader, in whichever country he may reside, that it is important to seek out a qualified coach or instructor of the official governing body of that country. In doing so there is a certain guarantee that he will be getting proper tuition. There are unfortunately many people around the world who purport to be teachers of judo but do not have any recognised qualification.

QUALIFICATIONS

Just because a person wears a Dan grade is or has been a leading competitor, it do not necessarily follow that he is a good i structor. His own personal experience an knowledge should ordinarily stand him good stead – but he may not have the ability impart that knowledge. This is where qua fications are useful. In passing examination and gaining qualifications such a person v learn teaching methods which enable him pass on that knowledge. But, and this is a ve big 'but', there is the other side to the co Just because a person has had the time an wherewithal to collect a handful of diplom and certificates but only has a certain level experience, his teaching will be limited to th level. My advice to the beginner therefore spend a bit of time looking into the bac ground of the coach you are considering. Fi out for yourself what he has done in judo. Wh has he taught? Does he run a successful cla or club? Does he inspire? Can he motivat

It is possible that you may not be able to fir such a person in your immediate district, which case you should yourself be prepare to travel. This is what all the great champio have had to do. When the most renowne T. P. Leggett taught at the Budokwai in Lo don in the 1950s and early 1960s, judo from as far afield as Bristol, Edinburgh, Ma chester and Glasgow would travel eve weekend to obtain the benefit of his teachir – and they were the days when there we ry few motorways.

Few judo instructors can teach at all levels. is is not always the instructor's fault. It is ually because he or she has only been owed to teach at one certain level. It is only the very large clubs where an instructor has e opportunity to teach at levels from begin- r to advanced. In the local evening institute ass, the instructor's hours are limited and, cause there is a steady stream of begin- rs, he is obliged to cater constantly at the vel of the majority. Consequently, he usually ses the more experienced who either move to the larger clubs or give up altogether cause they have become bored with the petition of beginner material. When an in- ructor becomes fully professional and his elihood depends on it, then he finds he must able to teach at all levels – unless of course is a National Squad Coach or National am Manager. In this category there are ose who only teach at that very high level. A mistake often made by club committees, my opinion, when considering the employ- ent or appointment of an instructor, is that ey tend to give a beginner class to the least perienced instructor. It is my firm belief that e beginner should be taught by the best structor in the club. It is in those formative onths when the basic ground rules are arned. If in that period a beginner develops a ad habit, it will be very difficult or sometimes possible to eradicate that bad habit later. ith the good and experienced instructor the eginner will be given the opportunity to study the major techniques in the *gokyu* on which e can build later, and not just the 'knock- wn' low-score actions.

HINTS AND ADVICE FOR JUDO INSTRUCTORS

As has been pointed out, the judo instructor must have the ability to inspire and motivate his or her students. A good instructor will be firm and critical, but he should temper this with reason, understanding and, where it is war- ranted, encouragement. In his enthusiasm to do a good job the inexperienced instructor or coach will tend to overteach. He will soon find that he is governed by the ability of his stu- dents and by how much they are able to absorb. Some of the best instructors I have known can spend an entire session teaching just one technique. Their secret has been that they use it and re-introduce it in so many attractive and fascinating ways that the class has been thoroughly absorbed. It is most important that the attention of students is maintained throughout each session. The stu- dent should not become bored with long lec- tures or explanations. Explanation of such things as judo customs, etiquette, and so on should be given between physically exhaust- ing routines and in just sufficient time to allow the students to recover for the next physical effort.

Information is more easily understood and more readily accepted if it is planned and presented in a logical way. The old fashioned 'do as I say' philosophy just does not wash these days. The average person is sufficiently independent and just will not accept such dogma; they need to be given reasoned explanations.

The ex-competitor judo instructor comes into his own when techniques have to be demonstrated, but even he will find it useful to have back-up support. Sometimes he will find it useful to use one of the more prominent players in the club to demonstrate his match- winning technique. A good instructor should have the confidence to be able to do this and at the same time maintain overall control of his class. This is also where visual aids can be used, as long as they are used intelligently and appropriately. Videos and motorised cameras can be used effectively (as in the various series of photos in this book). It is through these means that the champion's match-winning technique can be recorded and used as examples. Children in particular love this aspect. They like to relate to the champion and will try to imitate his actions.

The good judo instructor should have a class plan or course programme for whatever group he is teaching. The plan will vary depending on the level of the group he is teaching, but whatever level he is teaching he must ensure that the main part of the judo session is devoted to the study of judo skill. It is so easy, particularly where children are concerned, to want to be the popular tutor by allowing the pupils to play games rather than study skill acquisition.

Training games in the dojo became popular some years ago and can be useful to the overall training plan, but they can be overdone. Just as with the mobility exercises, training games should cover no more than 15 minutes in a normal 1½ or 2 hour session. Training games should also be closely related to judo and should not be allowed to get out of hand. A form of *Sumo,* for example, is good for teaching children or adult beginners how to deal with weight and balance, but the combatants should always be paired off equally weight for weight and size for size. British Bulldog is popular. It is a game where someone is selected (usually the senior grade) to stand in the middle of the dojo, and the others run from one end of the dojo to the other at a given signal. The person in the middle has to tackle someone and pin him on his back (usually for a short period of three to five seconds). The person pinned on his back successfully then joins and helps the original

person in the middle, and so on until only on in the group is left who is declared the winne This game teaches beginners to seize upc opportunities in groundwork, but as a game can get out of hand and become dangerou without certain ground rules and supervisio It is also another game which should be pla ed in groups of certain weight span.

When entering his first grading or contes the newcomer is confused by the signals ar calls of the referee if he has not becom familiar with them in the dojo. A good tip he is for the coach to use refereeing calls co stantly in the dojo, in this way the student soc becomes familiar with the calls.

Before taking a class, the judo instruct would be advised to make sure that adequa preparations have been made for the follov ing:

1. That each student has adequate clothir for judo activity. The hire of judo kit should n be encouraged, and it is such a reasonal priced garment that each person should po sess one. There are dangers in using ar other kind of clothing. The judogi is designe specifically for the heavy pulling and tuggir The instructor should also make sure th each person has been shown how to wear th judogi.
2. Check that a reasonable standard of mat available and that it is secure. Such chec should be made even on permanently la mats which the instructor might be famili with. He or she should check that no irregula ities have occured since the mat was la used. The mat area should be adequate f the number of students and a good rule thumb is two judoka to four square metres mat. If the mat is too crowded, the instruct should prepare his class plan according allowing one group to work on the mat and th other group sit on the side and study visu aids, contest rules, etc. Failing this he shou

st that another class is created.

The instructor should also check that all
sonable safeguards have been made with
ard the placing of the mat area and that
e is sufficient space between the mat
je and any furniture or fittings in the room or

Each student should be checked to ensure
t their judogi is clean, hands and feet are
an, finger and toe-nails pared, and that no
ellery is worn or metal objects are in the
. Long hair should be gathered back and
ured by a strong elastic band.

A first aid kit should be available and easily
essible, and the instructor should make
vision for any likely emergency situation
and ensure that there is easy access from the
mat area to the outside area where an ambu-
lance might easily be parked. The instructor
should enquire of all students of any physical
disability they may possess and be prepared
to act accordingly should any such disability
manifest itself during the judo session.

It is a good idea to have a blackboard and
chalk handy, and students should be encouraged to bring along to each session a pencil
and notebook. Hearing the judo terms and
seeing them written on the blackboard at the
same time helps the students to pick up the
terms quickly.

8 Judo as an Art

The demonstration of skills is artistic. Whatever the skill, there is a certain art form. The followers of cricket may wax enthusiastically about the forward defensive stroke of Geoff Boycott, the style of fast bowler Dennis Lillee, the poised balance of Graham Gooch, or perhaps the magnificent batting of Viv Richards. In the eyes of the enthusiast all of these things are artistic. It is the same in judo. We all remember those great moments when we have witnessed a brilliantly executed technique; to us this is the ultimate in artistic skill. Such incidents leave the throwing action imprinted on our minds forever. 'Do you remember so-and-so with his *harai-goshi* ?' is the kind of phrase you might hear when two judoka meet. Those great moments are sometimes encapsulated for all time on film, but they do not always happen in a major competition. Very often they happen in the dojo, but wherever it happens the thrill of witnessing such skill, such art, is never really forgotten.

KATA

We have heard much of randori and shiai, but there is a third aspect of judo which Kano was at pains to emphasise as being a most valuable part of judo training. This is called *kata*. Unfortunately, modern-day judo has concentrated on the development of contest skills and the competition champion, and as a result the all-round completion of the individual through kata has tended to be neglected. It seems that Kano was saying that the judoka must constantly strive to improve himself, for

the good of judo, for the good of himself, a for the good of others. To perfect one's m as well as one's body was one of his maxin and kata is intended to do just that.

Kata is a system of drills or pre-arrang forms. The Japanese hold great store in ka and it is not exclusive to judo. It can be fou in Japanese art, writing, architecture and fact anything expressing deportment and e quette. As a set of drills, we in the Weste world can see its value, but there is mu more to kata than that. Others might say th kata is a museum of all the judo techniqu but that is an over-simplification, for in kata can find many self-defence techniques wh would normally be too dangerous to do randori. The best known kata are as follow

Nage-no-kata – the kata of fifteen thro executed both right and left.
Katame-no-kata – the kata of holding ted niques, strangles and arm-locks.
Go-no-sen-no-kata – the kata of throws a their counter-throws.
Kime-no-kata – a kata depicting t Japanese style of self-defence.
Go-shin-jutsu – modern forms of s defence.
Ju-no-kata – a kata in which throws are c monstrated up to the point of *kake* and whe standing locks and strangles are performe (Note: this is a *kata* which need not be p formed on a judo mat).
Itsutsu-no-kata – an artistic presentation the five principle movements of the univers
Koshiki-no-kata – a kata of attack and c fence devised for men wearing Japane armour.